Books by Richard Perry

THE WORLD OF THE TIGER
THE WORLD OF THE POLAR BEAR
THE WORLD OF THE WALRUS
THE WORLD OF THE GIANT PANDA
THE WORLD OF THE JAGUAR
AT THE TURN OF THE TIDE
WATCHING SEA BIRDS
THE WATCHER AND THE RED DEER

The Many Worlds of Wildlife Series

THE UNKNOWN OCEAN
THE POLAR WORLDS
LIFE AT THE SEA'S FRONTIERS
LIFE IN FOREST AND JUNGLE
LIFE IN DESERT AND PLAIN

LIFE IN DESERT AND PLAIN

DESERT AND PLAIN

Richard Perry

Illustrated by Nancy Lou Gahan

VOLUME V: THE MANY WORLDS OF WILDLIFE SERIES

Taplinger Publishing Company   *New York*

First Edition
Published in the United States in 1977 by
TAPLINGER PUBLISHING CO., INC.
New York, New York

Copyright © 1977 by Richard Perry
Illustrations copyright © 1977 by Taplinger Publishing Co., Inc.
All rights reserved.
Printed in the United States by Vail-Ballou Press, Inc.

Published simultaneously in the Dominion of Canada by
Burns & MacEachern, Toronto

Library of Congress Catalog Card Number: 75-34733

ISBN 0-8008-4798-9

Designed by Mollie M. Torras

For Farah

ACKNOWLEDGMENTS

I have to acknowledge gratefully once again the essential research material provided by the Northumberland County Library Service at Morpeth and Alnwick, and also the following authors and publishers for quotations from their books: *Asia: A Natural History* by Pierre Pfeffer (Hamish Hamilton and Random House, 1968); *Forest, Steppe and Tundra* by Maud D. Haviland (Cambridge University Press, 1926); *Przewalski's Horse* by V. Zalensky (Hurst & Blackett, 1907); *Adaptation to Desert Environment: A Study on the Jerboa, Rat and Man* (Plenum and Butterworth, 1962); *Mammals of North America* by Victor H. Cahalane (Macmillan, New York, 1947, 1966); *Arctic Wild* by Lois Crisler (Harper & Brothers, 1958, 1973, and Secker & Warburg, 1959); *The North American Deserts* by Edmund C. Jaeger (Stanford University Press, 1957); *The Naturalist in La Plata* by W. H. Hudson (E. P. Dutton and J. M. Dent, 1923); *Australia and the Pacific Islands: A Natural History* by Allen Keast (Hamish Hamilton and

Random House, 1966); *A Territory of Birds* by Michael Sharland (Angus & Robertson, 1964); *A Glimpse of Eden* by Evelyn Ames (Houghton Mifflin, 1967, and Collins, 1968); *Return to the Wild* by Norman Carr (E. P. Dutton and Collins, 1962); *The White Impala: The Story of a Game Ranger* by Norman Carr (Collins, 1969); *Hunters and Hunted of the Savannah* by Felix Rodriguez de la Fuente (Orbis, 1971); *Innocent Killers* by Hugo and Jane van Lawick-Goodall (Collins, 1973, and Houghton Mifflin, 1974); *The Plains of Camdeboo* by Eve Palmer (Collins, 1966, and Viking, 1967); *Window onto Wilderness* by Anthony Cullen (East African Publishing House, 1969); *The Migratory Springboks of South Africa* by S. C. Cronwright-Schreiner (T. Fisher Unwin, 1925); *The Lion Hunter in South Africa* by Roualeyn George Gordon-Cumming (John Murray, 1856); *Animals of the African Year: The Ecology of East Africa* by Jane Burton (Holt, Rinehart & Winston and Peter Lowe, 1973); *Among the Elephants* by Ian and Oria Douglas-Hamilton (Collins & Harvill, 1965); *Serengeti: A Kingdom of Predators* by George B. Schaller (Knopf, 1972, and Collins, 1973); *The Long African Day* by Norman Myers (Macmillan, New York, 1972, and Cassell, 1973); *Out of Africa* by Isak Dinesen (Putnam, 1937, and Random House, 1938); *Wild Life in South Africa* by J. Stevenson-Hamilton (Cassell, 1947); *The Lost World of the Kalahari* by Laurens Van der Post (William Morrow and Hogarth Press, 1958); and to the Editor of *Wildlife* (formerly *Animals*) for permission to quote from articles by A. G. Bannikov, Michael Sharland, Graham Pizzey, Jane Goodall, David Houston, Dudley D'Ewes, and Norman Carr.

CONTENTS

ILLUSTRATIONS

Introduction

This volume in The Many Worlds of Wildlife series proved to be predominantly a search for the truth. Thus, on the one hand, the vast herds of buffalo and pronghorn antelope on the North American prairies, and those of the wild horses and asses on the Asian steppes, were decimated before they had been studied by competent naturalists. On the other hand, while several libraries of books and articles have been written during the past two hundred years about the incomparable wealth of animals on the African savannas, few of these give detailed information about the life histories of the larger mammals; and it is only within the past fifty years that this omission has been rectified to an almost overwhelming extent. Paradoxically, the more recent long-term field studies of such animals as lions, hyenas, hunting dogs, and some of the ungulates have tended to render the search for truth more instead of less difficult, because the behavior of, say, lions, varies widely from one habitat to another, with the result that certain forms of behavior become overemphasized.

The grasslands of Western Europe and the eastern United States are not natural, but have been converted by man from pristine forest and marsh to agricultural use. This is also true of the Indian savannas, which have been transformed from dry open woodlands to short-grass plains by deforestation and over-grazing by domestic stock. Earth's natural grasslands are ex-emplified by the Eurasian steppes, the prairies and pampas of the Americas, the plains and veld of East and South Africa, and the Australian downlands. They are predominantly transitional zones, merging into forest where the annual rainfall is higher, and into desert where it is lower. In temperate latitudes the endlessly rolling pastures of short grasses occur in the interiors of continents or in the lee of mountain ranges. In either case they are secluded from the moisture-laden sea winds, with the result that rainfall is slight throughout the year. Moreover, sum-mers are hot and winters cold, stunting most vegetative growth, with trees restricted to riverbanks and lake shores. Ivan Sander-son has likened these grass steppes to temperate deserts, whose characteristic daily and seasonal extremes of heat and cold they share.

By contrast, the tropical savannas—located around 35°N and 30°S—of East and South Africa in particular, but also of north-ern Australia and the South American llanos and campos, enjoy relatively high temperatures (above 64° F) at all seasons, with heavy but erratic rains during the summer months. These con-ditions favor a dominant vegetation of tall coarse grasses, which may grow to a height of 10 feet or more; and the savannas are studded with flat-topped trees, widely spaced so that each can trap sufficient moisture during the winter drought.

Because in both temperate and tropical grassland zones the rainfall is erratic, drought is an ever-present threat to perennial herbs, but the fibrous root masses of grasses can maintain their hold in the parched soil during prolonged drought and spring to life quickly when rain does fall. Moreover, they are resistant to the regular hazard of fire, with the seeds of some species able to survive beneath a charred layer of soil. They can also withstand, and indeed thrive on, intensive grazing because their bottom leaves lie flush with the ground, and the grasslands have evolved in association with the wild ungulates. Finally, most grasses are wind-pollinated, or reproduce by means of runners, and are therefore independent of pollinating insects, for which the plains tend to be too dry and windswept.

RICHARD PERRY

Northumberland, 1976

1: Birds and Burrowers of the Steppes

Before their agricultural exploitation the steppes—the most extensive natural grasslands in the world—stretched almost continuously in a 500-mile-wide fairway for 2500 miles from the black-earth plains, the *puzstas* of Hungary, through the Ukraine and southern Russia to the Altai in Mongolia, merging into the forest and swamp belts in the north and bounded by the Black Sea, the Caspian, and the mountainous deserts of Central Asia in the south. But wherever there were highlands or rivers, associated with an increase in rainfall, there were woodlands, while even slight undulations in the terrain encouraged the growth of low bushes such as spireas, laburnum, and broad belts of shimmering peach-red dwarf almond. As Pierre Pfeffer has pointed out in *Asia: A Natural History:*

> These shrubs are important in the evolution of steppe landscape for they hold the snow in winter and thus increase the humidity of the soil. This permits the forest to conquer the

steppe by progressive colonisation of such areas. The first trees to appear are the wild apples and pears, then the birches, and last, the oaks.

In this manner, forest islands, prolonging the wooded steppe and creating an intermediate zone between forest and prairie, are formed. This zone is almost evenly divided between grass-covered and tree-covered areas. The dominant element in Asia is the birch, while west of the Urals it is the oak. In western Siberia, the birch woods form circular clumps that alternate with prairies of the same size to give the land, as seen from an airplane, the appearance of a checkerboard.

It is in these wooded hollows that birds are most numerous, and that enterprising steppe and tundra naturalist, Maud D. Haviland, has described in *Forest, Steppe and Tundra* how in the early years of this century on the Russian steppe quail abounded wherever the herbage was high enough to afford covert:

> Their monotonous call, like the flick of a whiplash, resounds from dawn to dusk when the nightjars come forth to skim and *churr* over the flower fields. Hoopoes are common in such places, and the bramble brakes harbour a few warblers. Wherever there is sufficient tree growth, golden orioles and shrikes settle and breed; and serins, goldfinches, and linnets make these coppices their headquarters.

But over the greater part of the steppes the annual rainfall of between 10 and 30 inches is only sufficient to support grasses and tuberose plants. From February onward, as the snow melts, the fragments of uncultivated steppe or *stipa* surviving around the Black Sea and on the legendary Kirghiz are spangled with meadow saffron, crocuses, grape hyacinths, two-leaved squills, whitlow grass, and gagea resembling a yellow star-of-Bethlehem. They are followed, after the middle of April, by the tulips—white, yellow, dark red, white, and red—springing up singly at first and then in multitudes together over all the steppe. Once the tulips have flowered, blue and yellow lilies, in separate blocks or mingled, predominate over wide tracts of hillside, valley, and marsh; and in the early summer the steppes are gay with yellow, purple, and blue dwarf iris, with the blue sage and purple, white, and pink anemones, with the reds and scarlets of pheasant's-eye and with great sweeps of magenta or dark red fern-leaf peonies. But this profusion of multicolored flowering plants blooms only until the summer drought sets in at the end of June. During July and August the silvery-gray sea of knee-high or head-high feather grasses wither and crumple in the wind, and their place is taken by wormwoods and other shrubby xerophilous plants able to withstand heat and drought, with only the large red balls of the steppe thistle standing erect, until the grass shoots again just before the first snows in November and all the steppe is emerald green.

The lives of the animals inhabiting the steppe are governed by its climatic extremes, only less severe than those in polar and desert regions. The fierce sun, searing winds, and drought of the summers contrast with the harshness of the winters, when the steppes may be snowbound for weeks or months, and blizzards or *burans* rage with hurricane fury for two or three days at a time without intermission. During one such *buran* the Central Asia explorer, Douglas Carruthers, witnessed "the awe-inspiring spectacle of a stormy sea, whipped into violent commotion, freeze solid whilst in movement." This was Ebi Nor—the Wind Lake—situated at one entrance to the Dzungarian Gate, 46 miles long and 6 miles wide at the narrowest point, which links southern Siberia with Dzungaria, and is the only gateway through the mountain barrier between the Mongolian plateau and the great plain of northwest Asia.

Because of the overall uniformity of the steppe terrain, associated with a general lack of covert, both mammals and birds are exposed not only to all weathers, but also to predators. There are few trees or crags for large birds to nest on, while small birds such as the numerous species of larks, chats, and wheatears, must do so under clods or stones, and others—sand martins, bee-eaters, rollers, hoopoes, and rosy pastors—make use of holes or heaps of stones, while also serve as refuges from predators and shelter from the noonday sun. Both *puzsta* and steppe, however, swarm with beetles and also grasshoppers—"of all sizes, colours, and powers of flight, which spring up in all directions from the herbage, from great locusts that whizz away like snipe for a hundred yards or more, to little crickets," wrote Maud Haviland. There is indeed a breeding ground of locusts in the hinterland northwest of the Black Sea. Insect-eating falcons, especially kestrels and lesser kestrels, red-footed falcons, and hobbies are therefore numerous on the steppes, and a dozen of the smaller falcons may be seen hawking or performing aerial maneuvers at one time. Maud Haviland has described how, where a road or railway crossed the Russian steppe, red-footed falcons were always to be seen perched on the attendant telegraph wires, poised for instant pursuit of grasshoppers and other insects in the grass below:

> Their neighbours on these occasions are the rollers . . . conspicuously coloured blue and brown. The roller . . . usually sits motionless . . . from time to time dropping awkwardly down upon an insect. Its success is sometimes baulked by the falcon, which swoops down and carries off the prey from under its bill.

Small flocks of the slim green, brown, and primrose bee-eaters are also common on the Russian steppe, hawking like swallows after the insects flushed by the companies of rooks while turning over the dung of the grazing herds of horses and cattle. "Before a storm," wrote Maud Haviland, "the bee-eaters become intoxicated with excitement. As the clouds bank up, the birds gather into a flock, and rise almost out of sight in a mazy dance, while the steppe rings with their liquid cries."

For herbivorous mammals there is an abundance of grass and plant food on the steppes, but to take advantage of this most must be able to avoid the extremes of summer heat and winter cold, and also evade predators. Antelope, gazelles, and equines can escape the former by emigrating and the latter by their fleetness of foot. Some of the smaller mammals can also escape from predators by their agility. Those Siberian mice, the "jumping rabbits," are reputed to spring over the ground faster than a horseman, and the jerboas—those miniature "kangaroos" weighing only a few ounces—at 35 miles per hour. Obtaining a purchase on the sand with the dense mat of stiff hairs on the soles of their feet, they leap in 3-foot bounds on hind legs almost two-thirds of their body length, with fantastically long, hair-fringed, and tufted tails stretched out as "rudders."

The majority of small mammals overcome the problems of life on the steppe by burrowing, and dominant are the burrowing rodents, of which 4 square miles of steppe may hold as many as 325,000 but, in contrast, only 4 saiga antelope. Since this population of rodents eats upward of 2 tons of grass, bulbs, and tubers daily throughout the spring and summer, in comparison with the antelopes' 40 pounds, it is they and not the ungulates that are the main consumers of the steppe pastures. Most of them escape the winter frosts and snowstorms by retreating underground and, in many cases, hibernating after laying in stores of food during the summer. Among these are the ground squirrels, which include the marmots and susliks.

The brown bobac marmots—now almost extinct on the Russian steppe—live in large scattered communities, which may contain from fifty to several hundred burrows, each housing up

Bobac marmots of the steppe

to fifteen marmots. Despite the fact that frost on the steppe penetrates to a depth of 6 feet, most burrows are only from 5 to 7 feet deep, though a single burrow may give access to 200 feet of tunnels. Since 3½ cubic feet of soil are excavated from each burrow every year, the steppes in days gone by were studded with grass-covered mounds of spoil 2 or 3 feet high. After storing their burrows with grass and other vegetation for food and bedding, the marmots go into hibernation in September, plugging up the entrances with grass, twigs, and damp earth, and remain underground until March without losing much fat, though they may subsequently starve if the spring flush of grass is retarded.

The hibernatory period of the susliks or spotted ground squirrels (half the size of the bobacs), whose range extends from the *puzsta* to eastern Asia, illustrates the environmental problems of steppe dwellers, since it is even longer than that of the marmots, extending from late June, when the vegetation withers, to late March or early April the following year. Moreover, since they become torpid and aestivate during summer droughts, they actually remain underground for three-quarters of every year or longer! Before going into hibernation and sealing up the entrances with spoil, they transport quantities of seeds in their cheek pouches to storerooms in the vertical shafts of their burrows, but nevertheless lose three-quarters of their fat during this prolonged hibernation. In order to rear young they are obliged to mate almost immediately after emerging in the spring, and have time for only one litter; but although almost 75 percent of the three to eleven young do not survive their first year, while those that survive have a maximum life-span of only three years, the susliks are extremely numerous. Their colonies formerly covered thousands of square miles in densities of sixty-five to two hundred burrows to the acre, and it has been estimated that in the course of a few years a square mile's population of susliks excavates some 40,000 cubic yards of soil.

Some small rodents are also to survive the steppe winter without going into hibernation, though they store fodder in their burrows. The Daurian pikas—appropriately named mouse hares or piping hares—which live in coarse long grass near water in Mongolia and Siberia, collect the leaves of iris, cinquefoil, and wormwood for winter feed and even make hay, cutting piles of grass which they cure in the sun, and which are often eaten by gazelles. The mouse-sized gerbils in Turkestan's Kara Kum Desert are haymakers too, piling up quantities of grass and sedge to dry in diminutive haycocks near the entrances to their burrows, and actually preventing these from blowing away by pinning them to the sand with 2-inch pegs of milk vetch. The various species of steppe voles also do not hibernate, though during the winter they subsist on stores of bulbs and roots in burrows several feet underground, adapting themselves to a subterranean existence like the mole rats, which store dandelion and chicory roots in networks of winding tunnels. These the latter excavate to a depth of 16 feet with their powerful incisor teeth, in contrast to true moles which dig with their shovel-like forefeet and constantly extend the tunnels in their search for roots which, since they have no external eyes—or ears—they locate by touch with their blunt snouts.

Although the female voles are sexually mature when only six weeks old (and the males at an even earlier age), and are capable of producing six litters of from three to seven young between April and early October, it is suggested that their sporadic mass dispersals from their home range and the subsequent crashes in their numbers, following upon a population explosion, are not the result of a scarcity of food and certainly not of predation but, as in the case of the tundra lemmings, of overcrowding stresses on their hormone production. The populations of both common and sagebrush voles, for example, reach a peak every four or five years and are followed by a crash the succeeding year, when perhaps an imbalance in their hormones results directly in death or prevents the females from secreting sufficient milk for their young. Nevertheless a succession of food-abundant years must lead to an abnormal increase in the vole population, and a subsequent shortage of food and mass death or emigration.

Because of their numbers and constant gnawing and nibbling at plants and roots, the voles influence the ecology of the steppes more fundamentally than do the marmots and susliks. In peak years they may so denude the vegetation that a steppe may be pockmarked with bare patches, on which grow weeds that are unpalatable both to them and to the herds of antelopes and equines. Only after their numbers have been decimated do the grass and herbs begin to grow again. However, their incessant tunneling, together with the "deep plowing" by marmots and susliks excavating their burrows, are essential to the permanent fertility of the steppes. François Bourlière and Pfeffer have pointed out that by throwing up earth, whose composition generally differs from the topsoil, marmots and susliks assist in diversifying the vegetation. On the black-earth plains, for instance, the light soil thrown up by the bobac marmots is rich in calcium carbonate, essential to the seeds, deposited in bird droppings, of certain plants. In the more arid brown earth of the southern steppes, the spoil thrown up by the susliks is more saline than the topsoil, with the result that salt-tolerant plants, such as the black wormwood, habitually grows on suslik land. Conversely, in regions where the topsoil is brackish, the susliks help to purify it by bringing up salt-free earth from the lower levels, and thus producing a soil suitable for palatable meadow grasses.

The only relatively small steppe mammal that does not burrow is one of the world's more remarkable animals—the brown hare, whose global range over woodlands, arable fields, and pasture, heath, moor, steppe, and even desert stretches across Eurasia from Britain to the east coast of China, and from North Africa to the Cape. Brown hares are mainly solitary animals, unlike their relatives the mountain and Arctic hares, though in his *Rural Rides*, written in 1830, William Cobbett refers to great companies of hares on England's Wiltshire downs, while in our day they have formed the strange habit of gathering in scores or hundreds on airfields, not to graze on the acres of greensward but attracted apparently by the noise or vibrations of the air-craft, since they are also excited by thunder. But normally they are gregarious only during the mating season which, though popularly falling in March, actually extends from December and on through the spring into the summer. On odd days from March until May and even June half a dozen or more than a dozen hares will collect together at a traditional trysting place in field or steppe, perhaps to skip around and box each other tenta-tively, but sometimes to fight savagely, for not only do bucks fight with bucks, but also with the rather larger does if the latter are not ready to mate. Rearing up on their hind legs they box swiftly and vigorously with their forefeet and, if one contestant does not break away, leap into the air and strike with their hind feet at each other's bellies.

How have the brown hares been able to survive the harsh conditions of life on the steppes? Feeding on all kinds of vegeta-tion they, like rabbits and pikas, extract the maximum nourish-ment from their food by the practice of refection, in which the first pellets to be excreted are swallowed and redigested, proba-bly when they are resting in their "forms," but when excreted a second time they are left lying untouched. This process is not very different from that of cattle and sheep chewing the cud of undigested food regurgitated from their stomachs back into their mouths. In severe winters, however, when they are reduced to nibbling at withered grass stems or gnawing bark, large numbers of both adults and juveniles may die of starvation or from food poisoning as a result of eating the bark of broom, when this is the only greenery protruding above deep snow, because broom, like laburnum, contains the toxic alkaloids cystisine and sparteine, and though virtually immune to such viruses as myxomatosis, hare populations fluctuate widely.

Even during the hardest winter on the most exposed steppe, the hares do not apparently attempt to burrow but lie out in depressions in tufts of grass, selected to command a panoramic view, shelter from the wind, shade in the summer, and as much sun as possible on winter days. They are protected by an outer coat of coarse guard hair and dense woolly underfur against all weathers except the heaviest and most continuous rain, though allowing themselves to be buried beneath a heavy fall of snow, which renders them more or less immobile, and remaining under the snow for some days, reportedly in a semitorpid condition.

In preparation for such a Spartan existence the litters of from one to five leverets are born fully furred with eyes and ears open, in contrast to young rabbits, naked, blind, and deaf in the security of their burrows. In their exposed habitat the leverets are particularly vulnerable to predation by foxes, stoats, and polecats, though this vulnerability is countered to some extent by the habit of most does of dispersing their litters shortly after birth, carrying them by the scruffs of their necks, as a cat does her kittens, to separate forms not too distant from their own. Opinions differ as to whether the doe suckles them individually in their various forms or calls them together for this purpose, but after a lactation of probably three or four weeks, they become independent of her and go their own ways.

By this time they are almost safe from attacks by predators, being remarkably skillful at evading pursuit and able to turn in their own length when at full stretch at near 30 miles per hour, to leap broad ditches and fences 5 feet high and also to swim rivers and lakes. Moreover, the placement setting of their large eyes at the side of the head gives them a wide field of view, which they increase by standing up on their hind legs. However, when running away they tend to look backward and are likely to blunder into obstacles, while, like so many prey animals, they have difficulty in detecting and evaluating stationary objects—a hare will lope leisurely up a path to feed within 30 feet of such a large object as a man standing motionless—and this failing may render them vulnerable to stalking predators such as foxes. Hares, like rabbits and rodents, also possess a nostril pad covered with minute pimples and ridges that may serve as some form of receptor, and the characteristic habit of both hares and rabbits of "winking" their noses, and thus alternately exposing and concealing this pad, may be associated with the act of picking up airborne scents.

2: Wild Horses, Asses, and Antelope

Although vast areas of steppe, particularly in the Ukraine and north of the Caspian, have been plowed up and cultivated during recent decades, there are still sufficient virgin grasslands to support large numbers of ungulates, and these grass steppes were the natural home of millions of antelope, gazelles, wild asses, and horses. However, we are not likely ever again to see large herds of wild horses on the steppes. As late as the eighteenth century a race of wild horses, known as tarpans, ranged across the steppes from Poland in the west to beyond Lake Baikal in the east, and they were still quite numerous west of the Dnieper during the first half of the nineteenth century; but as a result of the ever-increasing agricultural exploitation of the steppes and the slaughter by farmers of the tarpan stallions, which frequently attacked domestic stallions when abducting their mares, the last of these wild horses were killed toward the end of the 1870s, though one survived in captivity until 1918 or 1919.

We know little about the tarpans except that there was a gray steppe breed and possibly a smaller forest breed which was almost white in its winter coat, but current reports by Mongolian zoologists suggest that a number, probably less than fifty, of another slightly larger race, the takh, better known as Przewalski's horse, still survive in at least eight localities in the rift, 200 miles long and 125 miles wide, between the ranges of Baitag-bogd and Takhiyn Shaara nuru (The Mountain of the Yellow Horses) in Dzungaria, where the Polish explorer N. M. Przewalski saw herds of from ten to fifty in the 1870s, and to which they have been confined exclusively since the end of the nineteenth century. Although they were still being hunted by frontier guards in the marches between Mongolia and Sinkiang as recently as 1949, the critical factor in their extermination has been the ever-extending range of the Mongolian nomads and their herds, which, pasturing around the few water holes in the summer, have denied the shy takhs access to these and forced them to migrate during the dry season to the desert country of the Dzungarian Gobi, where oases are hundreds of miles apart, though they are able to obtain some water by scraping holes in brine pans.

Their daily and seasonal movements appear to have been governed by this need for water, without which they could not survive for longer than a few days. For eight or nine months of the year this was obtainable from snow and thaw pools, but the winter freeze-up on the high Gobi steppes drove them, and also the wild asses and antelope, down to lower valleys where the snow was not frozen. Their habitat, at an altitude of 3000 to 4500 feet, comprised saline steppe, rocky ravines, and stony and sandy steppe desert, with their sparse vegetation of salt-impregnated shrubs, tamarisk, wormwood, feather grasses, rhubarb, and tulips. All were eaten by the takhs, grazing and drinking at night, resting during the day on some open flat, treading out deep tracks as they traveled in single file between grazing grounds and resting places. They frequented in particular stretches where the dominant vegetation was the saxaul, the most characteristic shrub of the Central Asian steppes, with minute leaves, fleshy fruit, and juicy bark which may possibly contain a reservoir of water. With roots extending for 20 or 30 feet belowground in search of moisture, the saxaul can make considerable though very slow growth in pure sand, reaching a height of 20 feet and forming small woods or even forests covering several miles; and since it can be coppiced, sprouting from the stub if felled after about fifty years, could be employed to stabilize areas of the sand dunes in southwestern Mongolia and Sinkiang.

Again, we know very little about the habits and herd structure of these wild ponies, only 12 or 13 hands high, with their short erect manes 6 or 8 inches long but tails reaching almost to the ground, and in most cases that hallmark of ancient lineage, a broad dark stripe along their spines. They are variously described as being colored dun, gray, yellow, and bright dark bay or, alternatively, of having a yellowish coat during the four months of summer and a much longer, dark chestnut-brown coat during the eight months of winter. There were perhaps two color types. Their most notable feature was a box-shaped head, reportedly housing a brain considerably larger than that of a tarpan, with which they may possibly have interbred, or of any domestic breed of horse. Although the observations of Przewalski, Alfred Brehm, and other nineteenth-century explorers are confused and contradictory, and those of some later writers equally so, it would appear that the stallions controlled harems of half a dozen or a dozen mares and their foals, though the leading mare might determine the time and direction of the herd's daily movements. The foals were born between late April and early June after the herds had returned from their wintering grounds to their summer pastures. According to Brehm, unsuccessful stallions were driven out of the herds during the mating season:

> For hours at this season [the latter] stand on the crests of the steep ridges . . . with their eyes on the valley before them. As soon as the banished one sees another stallion, he rushes down at full gallop, and fights to exhaustion with both teeth and hoofs.

At the conclusion of the rut the various harems collected in herds of a thousand or more and migrated to their wintering grounds on the Takhiyn Shaara nuru.

A Russian zoologist, Grshimailo (quoted by V. Zalensky in *Przewalski's Horse*), has described the dominance exercised by the stallions over their harems. On a stallion scenting mounted hunters he would alert his harem by snorting:

> At once they were off in single file, a young colt in the lead and the foals in the middle between the mares. As long as the herd was on the move and the hunters were to the side, so the stallion stayed to that side and kept his herd going in the direction he had chosen by using his head or forelegs to guide them. As soon as the horses had broken through the chain of hunters who now hunted them from behind, so the stallion changed his position and was now on guard in the van and in the way of those following him. He tried to drive on a tiny foal which could not reach the others on its weak legs . . . the dam tried to encourage it by whinnying softly to it. When she saw that this did not help, she left the herd. . . . But . . . with two forceful blows of his hoofs [the stallion] made

her gallop back to the herd and himself undertook the care of the foal. At first he pushed it along with his nose, then he seized it by the withers and pulled it along, and then he tried to animate it by seizing it and throwing it into the air.

The daily activities of the Central Asian wild asses or kulans of Kazakhstan and the Gobi Desert, and also the timetable of their migrations and the precise location of their summer pastures, are also governed by the availability of water, though to a lesser extent than in the case of the takhs; and because of their ability to subsist on the sparse wormwood and thornbush vegetation of desert regions as effectively as on the grass and herbs of the steppes, they have survived both hunting and the taking-over of their water holes by the nomads and their herds more successfully than the takhs. Thus although they were believed at one time to have been exterminated on the steppes of Kazakhstan and Mongolia before the end of the nineteenth century, this was happily not the case in the east, and herds of several hundred, including large numbers of foals, were encountered in southwest Mongolia as recently as 1972, and they have also extended their range in the Gobi.

In the spring, when the herbage is sappy and they are grazing for eleven or fifteen hours a day on more than a hundred varieties of grasses, plants, and shrubs, though especially on cereals and wormwoods, their water requirements are minimal. Indeed, the Third Asiatic Expedition of 1923–24, led by Roy Chapman Andrews, which camped for five weeks on the banks of a sizable lake in the center of the Gobi, found no evidence that the kulans ever drank from it, and they were in fact more numerous in those parts of the desert where there was no water at all. But according to the Russian zoologist, A. G. Bannikov, as soon as the moisture content of the vegetation falls by half, the kulans of Kazakhstan migrate to new pastures situated within 6 to 12 miles of a water hole. At this they drank after dark, having grazed their way leisurely to it from shortly before sunset:

> Once the herd has settled in a watering place it always uses the same one, so that a well-trodden path develops usually leading from one shallow depression to another. The asses avoid narrow ravines, thick undergrowth, and reeds, but do not mind charging down quite steep slopes to get to the water itself. The herd is led by an old female and the rest follow in a line behind her. The male as a rule comes to the water last. Asses drinking in ones or twos hardly make any noise, but big herds announce their arrival over hundreds of yards by the drumming of their hooves and the occasional cry of a stallion rounding up stragglers. Down a sleep slope a herd like this will descend like a veritable avalanche, the drumming of their hooves merging with their noisy snorting.

In the summer they may have to travel scores of miles in search of springs, and during the winter, when sheltering from storms in ravines and gorges, may be 50 miles from the nearest water hole; according to Bannikov, they sense a coming storm ten or twelve hours before it breaks. In Central Asia herds of up to a thousand kulans formerly migrated several hundred miles into the deserts in August from their summer pastures on the steppes of southern Siberia and northern Kazakhstan, returning in April at the first indications of the spring thaw on the steppes; but those inhabiting the semideserts of Mongolia, where pasture was sparse in the autumn and snow fairly frequent in the winter, migrated north into the steppes of eastern Mongolia and Transbaikalia where there was always less snowfall and better grazing.

In the spring the harems of from three to fifteen mares would break up to foal on open plains, where no wolves could approach unseen to the foals, which lay about for the first few days after birth, though able to run at 25 miles per hour when seven or ten days old. While the mares suckled their foals, the stallions wandered off on their own or with their almost invariable companions, the goitered or Gobi gazelles, which ranged over a great part of Asia's steppes and deserts, and a solitary stallion would often graze and rest with a gazelle day after day. Prior to the rut in the summer, young stallions over the age of twelve months were driven away by the harem stallions, to join up with straying mares or to form bachelor herds led by an aging stallion evicted from his harem.

Wolves were the only predators on the steppes strong enough to pull down equines, but adult kulans, lightly built and long-legged, were too fleet-footed to be run down, since they could reputedly gallop for a mile or more at 40 or 45 miles per hour,

The kulans—wild asses of Central Asia

before slowing down to a steady 35 miles per hour. One stallion indeed, when pursued in a car, averaged 30 miles per hour (including short dashes at 40 miles per hour when crossing in front of the car) over a distance of 16 miles, and was not finally brought to a halt, temporarily exhausted, until it had covered 29 miles. Their fleet-footedness gave the kulans a further advantage over the takhs, whose top speed was 30 miles per hour, though it is true that wolves would not attack a herd of takhs protected by a stallion, preying only on laggard, sick, or exhausted individuals.

If the steppes will never again have thousands of wild horses grazing over them, a remarkable calculated conservation program by the Russians has saved the most numerous of the steppes' larger fauna, the nomadic saiga—those yellow-brown, sheep-sized false antelope with long slender legs, the bucks of which bear short, amber-yellow, and slightly lyre-shaped horns. Despite the fact that the Russians had banned the hunting of saiga in 1919, they were believed to be near extinction by the late 1930s; yet by 1938 2 million were grazing over 1½ million square miles of the Soviet steppes, and by 1969 their numbers had been stabilized at about 1 million, 250,000 of which were concentrated between the Volga and Ural rivers. From this population a controlled kill of between 200,000 and 300,000 are now harvested annually.

The saigas' habitat is exclusively dry steppe or semidesert with a firm stony or clayey surface. Rough terrain is avoided because, although their peculiar shambling gait with heads held low enables them to reach speeds of up to 50 miles per hour on the flat, it prevents them from making sharp turns or from leaping even narrow ditches, though when ambling along leisurely they frequently jump high into the air to look for predators, which they can spot at a distance of 1000 yards. Thus they shun rocky ravines and valleys and also sandy areas, though during blizzards in severe winters they may seek shelter in the scrub growing on sandy hillocks and also in thickets of reeds, from feeding on which many succumb to gastroenteritis.

Like the chiru (the Tibetan antelope), saiga are distinguished by curiously swollen, proboscidean muzzles in which the small, widely spaced nostrils, directed downward, lead to a sac lined with mucous membrane. This device may serve to exclude sand when they are grazing, or to warm the cold steppe air or filter out wind-driven snow, but Bannikov suggests that its primary function is to counter the clouds of dust that envelop the lowered heads of the herds when running fast and far over steppe or desert. However, since the swelling is more developed in the bucks, whose "proboscises" become markedly extended before the rut, it must also be associated with some sexual significance.

Foraging across the steppes, the saiga feed on all the grasses and herbs, including, because they contain liquid, some that are poisonous to domestic stock. Indeed, so long as plants with a 65 percent moisture content are available, they do not require to drink; but when the moisture content falls in August, at a time when all surface water has dried up, they migrate in herds of from fifty to a thousand to lakes and rivers. At these they drink for eight or ten minutes in the morning, then graze their way 15 or 20 miles into the steppe, returning to drink again the next morning. In dry summers, however, poor pasturage and the absence of water may force them to undertake migrations of several hundred miles from their summer steppes, in the course of which they may travel 150 miles in a week. Bannikov has described one such migration on the Russian steppe in 1957 when, after a dry May, more than sixty thousand saiga ambled past his car in two days:

The tulips were no longer in flower on the steppe. The red and yellow patterns on their emerald carpets had given way to brown earth dotted with bluish-grey wormwood thickets. As dawn broke the trill of the larks and the loud song of the wheatears began to diminish, and the cautious pairs of demoiselle cranes, on the fresh patterns of green grass by the springs, looked attentively in our direction. A few hours later . . . a greyish-yellow ribbon of dust appeared in the trembling haze on the north-east horizon. . . . We could hear the ceaseless bleating of the young saiga and the answering responses of their mothers. . . . In the dust clouds we began to catch fleeting glimpses of saiga. . . . A continuous stream of animals flowed around our car. . . . From horizon to horizon the whole steppe suddenly seemed covered with them.

They were running unhurriedly, groups of them stopping here and there, and only at the car did they lower their heads—hook-nosed with soft, mobile proboscises—and increase their pace . . . occasionally some of them would leap up, raising their bodies almost vertical.

The saiga rut during a seven- or ten-day period in December—with the bucks contesting for harems of from two to fifty does—after they have migrated from the high steppes to their wintering grounds at lower altitudes. In open winters, when little snow has fallen on the high steppes, the does begin to migrate back in herds of tens of thousands to their traditional calving grounds on these as early as the end of March. According to Bannikov, the latter are located in saline semidesert or in the remotest parts of wormwood steppe where grass grows only sparsely and where there are no water holes and therefore no herds of domestic stock. The choice of these open flats with their wide field of view is also no doubt a defensive measure against wolves, for though the saiga, like the kulans, can normally outrun wolves, they are vulnerable when calving in twos or threes to the acre.

Saiga antelope, largest of the steppe's fauna

A more definite advantage of these flats is that there are bare patches on them, often the soft friable soil of suslik mounds. These warm up quickly in the sun and serve as couches on which the fawns—born all at one time in the course of a week in

May—can lie for their first twenty-four or forty-eight hours, though ten days after birth they are strong enough to migrate with the herds to the summer pastures. A yearling doe can bear a single fawn when only ten months old, a year before her own skeletal growth is complete, and two fawns when full grown. This precocious sexual maturity, together with a high fertility rate, must have been a major factor in the saigas' exceptionally rapid reestablishment of their former numbers on the Soviet steppes when assisted by conservation, for with about 80 percent of the fawns surviving the winter, and 40 percent of these until the following spring, a population of saiga can increase by 60 to 80 percent per annum.

A large proportion of the saigas' casualties in severe winters are adult bucks which, unlike the does, are not sexually mature until twenty months old and are apparently so debilitated by their exertions during the rut, when they graze hardly at all, though eating snow, that 90 or 95 percent of them may die in these conditions. Their dead and dying divert the attentions of wolves from the healthy does and yearlings. This restriction of heavy mortality to the polygamous bucks is a further factor assisting the rapid recovery of saiga populations, as perhaps has been the recent large-scale reduction in the numbers of wolves, which are, or were, extraordinarily numerous on the steppes and in semidesert regions, where the abundance of herbivores and the flat terrain offered easy hunting. In Kazakhstan alone more than two hundred thousand wolves have been officially destroyed in the past twenty years or so with the aid of helicopters and tracked vehicles. But saiga and wolves have existed side by side for thousands of years; only where a prey population has been reduced critically below its normal strength by some catastrophe can predators threaten its survival.

In very cold winters when, however, little snow falls on their wintering grounds, the saiga may be compelled by the freezing-up of all sources of water to return out of season to the high grass steppes in search of deep snow with which to quench their thirst; and every ten or twelve years there are excessively harsh winters, when strong cold winds rapidly compact the snow into a hard surface, rendering the procurement of food difficult. Moreover, a frozen snow cover only 2½ inches deep causes multiple wounds on the saigas' forelegs, preventing them from escaping wolves, as does deep snow. If these conditions are accentuated by a severe ground frost then, in Pfeffer's words, "animals spend an immense amount of time nibbling at plants to free them of their icy sheaths. As a result, an animal cannot get enough food in the course of a day to make up for the energy it expends."

Such frosts usually last for only one or two days, but if one persists it results in the *djout* or *dzud*, the death. If the frost extends over a wide area, 150,000 saiga can starve to death in a matter of weeks, particularly if they are in poor condition after a droughty summer, or are killed by wolves in the sheltered hollows of phoenix (poplar) trees, to which both they and the kulans retreat for shelter. When *djouts* occur at normal intervals of several years, animal populations can build up again; but if they occur in consecutive years, local populations of some species may be wiped out, as was the case, after a series of severe winters in the late 1940s and 1950s, with the goitered gazelles on the upper Yenisey steppe and possibly the kulans in Kazakhstan. However, if *djout* conditions are not too widespread, the greater part of the saiga population escapes local blizzards by migrating in immense herds of up to a hundred thousand and, traveling hundreds of miles in a few days, lose only 30 or 40 percent of their numbers, whereas the goitered gazelles, which migrate only short distances, suffer 80 or 90 percent losses. One may well ask why these gazelles should only migrate short distances? It is evident that deep snow not only hinders an animal's search for food, but also, when it is deeper than the animal's hind legs, must impede movement. Pfeffer has stated that the critical depth is from 24 to 28 inches for wild horses and asses, and 16 inches for both saiga and gazelles. He adds, however, that:

> The weight of an animal and the bearing surface of its hoofs must also be taken into account. The pressure on the snow amounts to 14 pounds per square inch for the wild ass, a little less for Przewalski's horse, about 6 pounds for the gazelle. . . . Since the adult wolf exerts a pressure of only 2 pounds, it can run easily across well-packed snow or snow covered with an icy crust that would collapse under the weight of any of the steppe ungulates.

3: Survival in Asian Deserts

It will have become apparent in the previous chapter that it is impracticable to draw a hard-and-fast line between the environment and fauna of the steppes and those of the adjacent semidesert. Indeed, the borderlines between steppe and semidesert and between semidesert and true desert fluctuate from year to year, and even from season to season, according to the vegetation's response to the erratic supply of water from melting snows and brief rains. Just as along their northern marches the grasslands of the western steppes merge into the well-watered parklands extending southward from the forest belt, so in the south the fertile black earth (10 feet deep in some regions) becomes increasingly deficient in lime. "Grasses become increasingly sparse," notes Pfeffer, "and marly, sandy or stony soil increasingly evident among the scattered tufts of vegetation;" in summer the bleached and blinding landscape shimmers with heat waves. As Maud Haviland pointed out:

The soil base is all-important. Where heavy enough to retain moisture, vegetation is abundant: but poor sandy soils support only desert-type plants, and where the southern borders of the artemisia steppe merges into sandy steppe . . . they are as parched and sterile as the desert itself for eight or nine months of the year, supporting only poor grasses, thistles, a few stunted thorn bushes and, characteristically, wormwoods (*Artemisia*).

The bitter fragrance of the black wormwood, whose roots may go down to a depth of 3 feet or more, dominates the artemisia steppe, and this black absinthe creates a black and white pattern over extensive areas of the sun-cracked crust of salty clay. During drought, when its leaves are concealed in the black stalks, the plant appears to be dead, but when rain falls the leaves spread and long stalks tipped with grayish flower clusters thrust up.

It is only a stride from the artemisia steppes into the flanking deserts that stretch unbroken, except for the Aral-Caspian depression and a few isolated mountains, through Iran and Afghanistan to the Gobi, whose longer axis extends from east to west between Inner and Outer Mongolia, for though stony and clayey deserts may be almost devoid of vegetation, some sandy deserts may, like the steppes, blossom into a brief but intensive spring with the first fall of rain, and become magically carpeted with meadow grasses and sedges, colored with blue Veronica, red poppies, yellow ranunculus, purple iris, blocks of tulips, and *Rheum tataricum*, a form of rhubarb known as the "camel's food," though grasses and plants alike are burned off by the scorching heat of the sun long before the onset of the summer drought.

A single violent rainstorm, delivering in a matter of minutes all the water that a particular section of desert may receive in a

year, is sufficient to germinate seeds that have long lain dormant, enabling them to grow, mature, and produce new seed in
as short a period as eight or ten days. Most of them are peren-
nials with a complex root system enabling them to survive in
soft sand, and they develop so rapidly because their growth
cycle begins in the autumn, though it is interrupted during the
winter months. However, as a contributor to *The Living World of
Animals* has stated:

> Towards the centre of great desert regions, rainfall becomes
> less and less frequent. Finally a region is reached where wind
> erosion has exceeded water erosion for so long that the land-
> scape has an almost lunar appearance. Here the abrasive
> wind-driven sand has smoothed, polished and moulded the
> surrounding rocks and hills into a variety of weird shapes and
> patterns.

The interior of the basin-shaped Gobi Desert, whose bottom
lies about 3000 feet above sea level, but its rim at nearly 5000
feet, comprises for example a succession of salt deserts and shifting sand dunes, interspersed with ancient valleys paved with
pebbles which the Mongols call *gobis*, and stretches of clay and
yellow-earth loess overlaid by black gravel resembling flat seg-
ments of shattered slates. It is so arid over large areas that
Przewalski traveled 1000 miles without encountering a single
stream:

> These sands beget a sort of stifling anguish of the spirit. If
> you climb one of these mounds [dunes] and survey space, no
> vegetation gladdens your eyes. You will not see a blade of
> grass, no animal except the lizard. The silence is unbroken
> even by the song of the crickets; you are lost in a sea of sand,
> surrounded by the quiet of the tomb.

But Przewalski's experience does not imply that because the
Gobi is a desert it is a faunal vacuum. On the contrary the

Third Asiatic Expedition encountered considerable numbers of kulans and goitered gazelles in the Central Gobi, and other travelers have reported the ubiquitous brown hares as being everywhere on the caravan trails and around old campsites, and have observed that only in the desert do they go to ground in burrows to escape the burning sun, though also sitting in the shade of a rock or bush, losing body heat through those long ears that are a characteristic feature of other desert animals, such as jerboas, fennecs, and foxes.

Moreover in the north, east, and southeast, the Gobi merges into broad belts of grassland that include riverine meadows with a short close growth of wild liquorice, and on these, once again, are the pikas and the familiar colonies of bobac marmots and susliks (preyed on by masked polecats), while large herds of Mongolian gazelles or zeren, whose golden-brown coats whiten in winter, replace the saiga on these eastern steppes, just as the goitered gazelles replace the zeren in the desert. Andrews encountered herds of from six thousand to eight thousand zeren, composed of does only, in the spring, migrating slowly to the flat plains where safer from the attacks of their main predators, the wolves, they dispersed to calve. The adults, which were capable of 50 miles per hour and possibly higher speeds in short spurts, were too fleet-footed to be run down by wolves in normal circumstances. In the autumn both does and bucks collected in even larger herds for the rut. The goitered gazelles, however, were never observed in large herds, probably because the sparse feeding in the desert prohibited such concentrations of grazing animals.

The environmental problems which the true desert dwellers must overcome or adapt to are the sparseness of vegetation, the total absence of water for periods of months or even years, and the extremes of temperature, which may rise to above 130° F in the shade and 160° F in the sun, and fall to 50° F or lower during the night. The short growing season of most desert plants also influences the life cycles of desert animals. Ungulates escape starvation by being constantly on the move, but the yellow race of susliks, which inhabit both clay steppe and desert, eat only the green parts of ephemeral plants, and therefore have a guaranteed food supply only from early March until late May. Animals that are diurnal require protection against the hot ground. Those lizards that run bipedally on their hind legs benefit by having their bodies raised above the heated layer of air at ground level. Sand grouse, on the other hand, can rest on the sand during the heat of the day because the skin on their underparts is thickened; furthermore, because the skin is not attached to the flesh, all parts of their bodies in contact with the ground are isolated by an air chamber. These protective devices are even well-developed in newly emerged chicks, which are hatched during the hottest season of the year and can run about over sand heated to 150° F. But as J. P. Kirmiz has pointed out in *Adaptation to Desert Environment:*

> The problem of the animal in the desert is not so much the intensity of the heat, which it can avoid by leading an underground and nocturnal life, as the scarcity of food and water. . . . In the natural order of desert factors, scarcity of water leads to rarity of food and the insufficiency of water and food obliges the animal to eat less.

Kalman Perk, in an article in *Animals*, stresses the paramount importance of water:

> If the environment is warmer than the body temperature, heat flows from the hot surroundings into the organism. Hence, to keep the body temperature from rising, excess heat must somehow be dissipated. As the only means of reducing body heat under these conditions is thought to be by evapora-

tion of water, the availability of water becomes, therefore, a vital matter. If there is no water supply, then it might be assumed that there would be no animal life.

But the varied inhabitants of the deserts have been able to adapt to the shortage of water. Sand grouse, which both feed and nest at a distance from water, are obliged to fly as far as 40 miles in the early morning or late evening or by moonlight to the nearest water hole; and from observations initially on captive and subsequently on wild birds, it would appear that cock sand grouse have a remarkable method of transporting liquid to their nestlings. On arriving in large flocks at a pool, the males, after rubbing their breasts violently on the ground and setting their feathers awry, walk belly-deep into the pool, crouch, ruffle, and rock their bodies until the breast feathers, which can soak and retain twice as much water as a normal bird's, are saturated. They then fly back to their nests, where the chicks drink by nibbling and drawing the wet feathers through their beaks, continually changing places until all moisture has been extracted. It is difficult to credit that the feathers of a sand grouse flying many miles through dry desert air could retain even a trace of moisture, but after flying 20 miles in hot weather, a cock is said to be able to deliver about half an ounce of water to its chicks; and it is a fact that while captive chicks die of thirst even when drinking water is available, they accept water from wet cotton. Prior to the hatching of the chicks, the saturated feathers of an adult returning from drinking to relieve its mate also serve to prevent the eggs from becoming overheated by dampening them and the soil around the nest. In a paper in the *Journal of Experimental Biology*, A. M. Rijke has explained the water-holding mechanism of the sand grouse's feathers:

Water applied to the ventral side [of a feather] is readily drawn up into the hair-like extensions of the barbules and when it reaches the basal, coiled regions the helices abruptly uncoil and proceed to expose their lengthy ends perpendicular to the plane of the feather. This arrangement of the barbules permits large quantities of water to be drawn up by capillary attraction. On subsequent drying the barbules will coil up again and intertwine with adjacent barbules, thus returning to the original feather structure.

Even on the steppes, marmots may have to rely for moisture on dew licked off grass stems. In the desert, rodents such as gerbils and jerboas probably never actually drink water, though that they have the instinct to do so is illustrated by the fact that in captivity jerboas lift water to their mouths with their tiny forefeet. In the natural state, however, they can obtain sufficient liquid from seeds, bulbs, tubers, and juicy plants, and also from insects, because they are equipped with hyperefficient kidneys that eliminate waste products by forming urine with a very low water content. Although even the driest seeds contain some absorbed water, it is from their ability to manufacture "metabolic" water—breaking down the starchy contents of the seeds into carbon dioxide and water—that the burrowing rodents of the desert derive just sufficient liquid to free them from the necessity of drinking, nor, since they can shelter in their burrows during the hottest part of the day, do they require to use water for heat regulation. As Knut Schmidt-Nielsen has said: "They are an ecological paradox, living in the desert without being exposed to the rigor of desert heat."

Although some hoofed animals are obliged to travel considerable distances in search of water, since they must drink every few days, the goitered gazelles are probably an exception to this rule, with the ability, like rodents, to reduce the amount of water dissipated in their urine; while the wild camels, the sandy-red havtagai, do not require to drink at all during the short season of green growth, providing that they do not travel too far or too fast, for according to Przewalski these, the only true wild camels, though able to trot very swiftly, lack the stamina of domestic camels and can be overtaken by them in long pursuits.

As in the case of the takhs, and to a lesser extent the kulans, observations on the havtagai in their natural habitat are few and conflicting. Thus according to one authority, they must have water every four or five days when the spring vegetation withers, and are less resistant to drought than domestic camels, being primarily steppe rather than desert animals, whereas according to another authority, even in the summer when dry camel bush (*Alhagi camelorum*), browsed by no other animal, is the only fodder available, they can survive for fourteen days or longer without water, browsing early in the morning and at dusk, and lying up during the heat of the day on vantage points bare of scrub. Since camels do not lose their appetite when deprived of water, until excessively dehydrated, their ability to thirst for such long periods enables them to forage over a much wider range than other desert animals.

In Przewalski's day the few wild camels still inhabiting the Lob Nor region to the south of Dzungaria migrated from the desert in the summer to montane valleys at altitudes of 11,000 feet or higher, where in addition to springs there was a more abundant supply of camel thorn, which in some districts they prefer to plants without thorns, together with their favorite *Hedysarum*, one of the pea-flower family; while according to Bourlière, those pasturing on the steppes move in the autumn to the dried-up beds of temporary streams in order to browse on the leaves of poplar trees. Przewalski was told by native herdsmen that the males fought savagely when rounding up harems of several dozen she-camels during the rut in January and February, and that the young were born in March every third year.

We know that domestic camels, and also donkeys, are capable of traveling 300 miles over sand dunes in ten days and, if fresh grazing is available, 600 miles in twenty-one days, without watering, though losing more than a quarter of their weight in the form of fat stored mainly in the hump, and subsequently refueling with a single prodigious drink of 20 or 25 gallons. Indeed, H. H. Finlayson records that, after traveling 537 miles in thirty-four days in very hot weather over the semidesert of Australia's Red Centre, his camel drank 33 gallons, measured by buckets, and a further 10 gallons after the lapse of a quarter of an hour. Although camels do not in fact store water either in their humps or in their stomachs, they do have the unique ability to retain water in the bloodstream. Moreover, they can endure a body temperature rise of several degrees before they begin to lose fluid by sweating and expiration, while after cooling off during the night they can bear great heat during the day, since they are insulated to some extent by the hair and fat on their backs.

The havtagai which, like domestic camels, have long lashes to shade their eyes from the sun's glare, nostrils that can be closed against wind-driven sand, and two toes linked by pads that spread their weight over the shifting sand, differ from them in being uniformly sandy-colored, whereas domestic camels may also be dark brown, black, or even white. They differ also in their longer though fine-boned legs (lacking callosities) and small feet and pads that leave a footprint about half the size of a domestic camel's, in the thinner texture of their coats and the absence of mane and beard, and in their humps, which are small pointed cones and invariably firm, in contrast to those of domestic camels, which vary in size and condition according to their owner's health.

In the late 1950s it was believed that the wild havtagai had been exterminated and that only feral herds derived from crosses with domestic camels remained; but although matings between wild bulls and domestic she-camels were often observed by the nomads, they stated that the latter invariably returned after mating to the domestic herds. Since the 1960s small herds, composed of two or more males with from three to five females, of what are believed to be purebred havtagai, have been sighted on the steppes at altitudes between 4800 and 6400 feet in the southwestern Gobi and in the Lob Nor region. The latest Mongolian reports indicate that their numbers have markedly increased with protection, aided by the fact that their grazing grounds lie outside those of the nomads' herds, and Bannikov estimates that there are now about nine hundred, including one herd of eighty with calves, ranging over some 15,440 square kilometers of the Transaltaian Gobi.

4: The Prairie Buffalo and Pronghorns

The North American plains and prairies, the counterpart of the Eurasian steppes, formerly extended from the deciduous forests of Pennsylvania and Ohio to the Rockies, and from Alberta almost to the Gulf of Mexico, with extensions in Washington east of the Cascade Mountains, and in Oregon, in the Great Valley in California, and in Arizona, New Mexico, and southwest Texas. Though now almost entirely given over to agriculture, their universal characteristic was the dominance of grasses, except in arid alkaline or sandy regions or those covered with sagebrush—the wormwood of the steppes. In the rich soils of the moister, low-lying eastern prairie with its moderate rainfall, tall grasses such as the big bluestem grew to a height of 10 or 12 feet and formed a dense, compact sod so tough that a plow required five yoke of oxen to break it up; on the drier prairie to the west grew the midgrasses; while the semiarid high plains and prairies were the domain of the short grasses such as the 12-

or 16-inch blue grama and the 4- or 5-inch buffalo grass. However, in the driest high prairies in the lee of the Rockies, these short grasses might achieve a growth of no more than 2 inches.

According to David E. Costello an acre of the tall grasses would produce up to 3000 pounds of forage—sufficient to feed one buffalo for more than two months—whereas several acres of the short grasses on the high prairie would only furnish half that amount. Nevertheless the latter which, in the words of Colonel Richard Irving Dodge, "formed a thick close mat of beautiful sward, green as emerald in the early spring, but of a yellowish-grey later in the season," did not dry up and wither like the tall grasses during the summer heat, but cured like mown hay and preserved their nutritive value throughout the fall and dry winter, providing the buffalo and pronghorn antelope with prime feed. In drought years, however, seasonal grass production might fall to less than 100 pounds of palatable forage per acre, which was barely enough to feed for three days a large bull, standing 6 feet at the shoulder and weighing a ton or considerably more; while several consecutive summers of drought must have devastated hundreds of square miles of prairie grasslands, since they were associated with prairie fires that ran for hundreds of miles, and with plagues of grasshoppers, concentrated in densities of more than a hundred to the square yard, that devoured all vegetation, including even the low-growing prickly pear. In his *Narrative of the Canadian Red River Exploring Expedition of 1857,* Henry Youle Hind has described the 1857 plague of locusts which cut down the prairie grass in the Souris River country to a uniform level of 1 inch above the ground:

> On the 2nd of July we observed the grasshoppers in full flight towards the north. They commenced their flight about nine in the morning, and continued until half-past three or four o'clock in the afternoon. About that hour they settled

around us in countless multitudes, and immediately clung to the leaves of grass. . . . On subsequent days, when crossing the great prairie . . . the hosts of grasshoppers were beyond all calculation; they appeared to be infinite in number. Early in the morning they fed upon the prairie grass, being always found most numerous in low wet places where the grass was long. As soon as the sun had evaporated the dew, they took short flights, and as the hour of nine approached, cloud after cloud would rise from the prairie and pursue their flight in the direction of the wind. . . . The number in the air seemed to be greatest about noon, and at times they appeared in such infinite swarms as to lessen perceptibly the light of the sun. The whole horizon wore an unearthly ashen hue from the light reflected by their transparent wings. The air was filled as with flakes of snow, and time after time clouds of these insects, forming a dense body casting a glimmering silver light, flew swiftly towards the north-north-east, at altitudes varying from 500 to 1000 feet and upwards.

Lying on my back and looking upwards as near to the sun as the light would permit, I saw the sky continually changing colour from blue to silver white, ash grey and lead colour, according to the numbers in the passing clouds of insects . . . the day being calm, the hum produced by the vibration of so many millions of wings . . . more resembled the noise popularly termed "a ringing in one's ears", than any other sound.

Contemporary evidence as to the ravages of prairie fires are conflicting. On the one hand Dodge, with thirty-four years' experience of the prairies in the middle years of the last century, stated that they were not as a rule violent enough to be dangerous to the herds of buffalo, which did not stampede but collected on unburned ground where the grass was untouched, whereas, according to Alexander Henry, fire not only destroyed the grazing but the buffalo themselves. In his *Journal* for November 25, 1804, we read for example:

Plains burned in every direction and blind Buffalo seen every moment wandering about. The poor beasts have all the hair singed off; even the skin in many places is shrivelled up and terribly burned, and their eyes are swollen and closed fast. It was really pitiful to see them staggering about, sometimes running afoul of a large stone, and other times tumbling down hill and falling into creeks, not yet frozen over. In one spot we found a whole herd lying dead.

So, too, Hind recounted in 1860 how:

Blind buffalo are frequently found accompanying herds, and sometimes they are met with alone. Their eyes have been destroyed by prairie fires; but their quickened sense of hearing and smell, and their increased alertness enable them to guard against danger, and makes it more difficult to approach them in quiet weather than those possessing sight. . . . When galloping over stony ground, blind buffalo frequently fall, but when quietly feeding they avoid the stones and boulders with wonderful skill.

It is reasonable to assume that it was the immense aggregations of buffalo, and those of the pronghorn antelope, split up into grazing herds of a few score or hundred, that maintained a matlike sward of turf over millions of acres of prairie. Whether the buffalo actually extended their range by creating new grasslands is disputed. According to some authorities there is no evidence that they did so, but others assert that the constant horning and rubbing of itchy heads destroyed even mature trees by stripping the bark off them, while small trees, shredded of their bark, became tinder-dry and burned with fury in the frequent prairie fires. Thus any regeneration of woods from seedlings was prevented, and grasses replaced the trees. It may well be that the original buffalo grazed in open woodlands as much as on the plains, for the extent of the latter was probably vastly increased by the enormous tracts of woodland burned down by the Indians, both when communicating by signal fires and when driving the buffalo herds into ravines or pounds from which there were no exits, and in which they could be slaughtered en masse.

The buffalo formerly ranged over the plains from a near-Arctic habitat around the Great Slave Lake, where they were represented by the wood buffalo, and over the eastern plains to a subtropical environment in Mexico, and across the continent from the Great Plains watered by the Mississippi, where their herds were concentrated in greatest numbers, to the Rockies. There are no reliable contemporary estimates of their numbers, and Ernest Seton's figure of between fifty and seventy-five mil-

The American prairie buffalo

lion grazing over between 300 and 500 million acres of plains, prairies, and forest is generally accepted as possible. The great herds had been decimated before Seton's time, but there are contemporary accounts of their magnitude. In *Narrative of a Journey across the Rocky Mountains*, the naturalist John K. Townsend describes the Platte River in May 1833:

> The whole plain, as far as the eye could discern, was covered by one enormous mass of buffalo. Our vision, at the very least computation, would certainly extend ten miles, and in the whole of this great space, including about eight miles in width from the bluffs to the river bank, there was apparently no vista in the incalculable multitude.

While six years later, when on the Santa Fe Trail, Thomas J. Farnham wrote in *Travels in the Great Western Plains, 1839* that:

> The buffalo during the last three days (June 21–24) had covered the country so completely, that it appeared oftentimes extremely dangerous even for the immense cavalcade of the Santa Fé traders to attempt to break its way through them. We travelled at the rate of 15 miles a day. The length of sight on either side of the trail, 15 miles; on both sides, 30 miles:— $15 \times 3 = 45 \times 30 = 1,350$ square miles of country, so thickly covered with these noble animals, that when viewed from a height, it scarcely afforded a sight of a square league of its surface.

Again, in July 1869, just before the final years of systematic extermination, Isaac Cowie, who was in the service of the Hudson's Bay Company from 1867–74, describes in *The Company of Adventures* how in Saskatchewan the buffalo blackened the whole country, their compact moving masses covering it so that not a glimpse of green grass could be seen:

> Our route took us into the midst of the herd, which opened in front and closed behind the train of carts . . . but always

leaving an open space about the width of the range of an Indian gun in front, rear and flanks. The earth trembled, day
and night, as they moved in billow-like battalions over the
undulations of the plain. Every drop of water in our way was
foul and yellow with their wallowings and excretions. So we
travelled among the multitude for several days . . . mar-
velling at its myriads and their passive indifference to us.

And in May, two years later, Dodge noted that when he
drove in a light wagon from old Fort Zara to Fort Larned on the
Arkansas, a distance of 34 miles:

At least twenty-five miles of that distance was through an immense herd. . . . The whole country appeared one great
mass of buffalo, moving slowly to the northward; and it was
only when actually among them that it could be ascertained
that the apparently solid mass was an agglomeration of countless small herds of from fifty to two hundred animals, separated from the surrounding herds by greater or lesser space.

It was perhaps only in 1970 when Frank Gilbert Roe published his critical study, *The North American Buffalo*, after fifteen
years' research, that it became fully apparent how much of the
buffalo's natural history had been distorted by various writers
trimming the facts to fall in with their own hypotheses as to
how the buffalo ought to have behaved. Such internationally
famous naturalists as W. T. Hornaday in particular, and also
Seton, neither of whom actually observed the original great
herds, are shown by Roe to have been most unreliable in some
of their reportage of buffalo lore and natural history, as have
some more recent authors. To get at the truth it is therefore necessary to return to original sources, which are mainly in the
form of incidental notes scattered throughout the numerous accounts of exploration and encounters with the various tribes of
Plains Indians.

Although tens of thousands of buffalo might be grazing over one section of prairie, these were, as we have seen, usually in self-contained herds and smaller groups. According to Dodge, most of the groups among the scattered herds contained more bulls than cows, since single bulls did not collect harems, and one grazing group would join amicably with another, when the bulls of the former group would take their places among the other bulls in their accustomed position on the flanks of the cows and calves. The latter were born on the summer pastures between the middle of April and late June (the majority in May) in a red coat that they retained for six months until molting into their winter coat, and they and the calving cows were protected from such predators as wolves in particular, but also coyotes and sometimes the plains grizzlies, by the bulls forming up around them. Indeed, in Dodge's experience, the cows frequently deserted their calves when harassed by wolves or hunters, and it was always the bulls that protected the calves. He quotes an experience of an army surgeon who was puzzled by the behavior of a group of six or eight bulls which were formed up in a close circle, heads facing outward, twelve or fifteen paces from another circle of a dozen wolves:

> After a few moments the knot broke up, and, still keeping in a compact mass, started on a trot for the main herd, some half a mile off. . . . The central . . . figure of this mass was a . . . little calf so newly born as scarcely to be able to walk. After going fifty or a hundred paces the calf laid down, the bulls disposed themselves in a circle as before, and the wolves, who had trotted along on each side . . . sat down . . . again.

A feature of the buffalo's daily life during the summer heat was the extensive use they made of wallows, though if mud and water were not available, a roll in the dust served. The bulls wallowed much more frequently than the cows, probably because, with their greater profusion of long shaggy hair on their foreparts, they suffered more from the heat, and also perhaps, as Seton suggested, because they became more heavily infested with prickly seeds such as those of the spear grass, which was known on the plains as the "wild oat" because the seeds, with their sharp corkscrew points and long barley-like awns set with fine backward-pointing bristles, resembled those of the oat. According to Seton, "When this contrivance touches the wool of a Buffalo, its barbs at once cling, and . . . it revolves seven or eight times in an hour, boring through the wool and finally reaching the skin. . . . It keeps on boring, even through the skin, till an angry irritating sore is produced."

It was Dodge's opinion that the wallows were in the first place natural phenomena caused by alternating heavy rains and hot sun producing impermeable depressions on the level prairie, and that these were enlarged in the spring when the buffalo, for lack of trees on which to rub off the remnants of their winter "wool," rolled on the ground and in these depressions. George Catlin, however—who in the years 1832–39 traveled thousands of miles over the plains in the course of visiting forty-eight Indian peoples and painting (not very well) more than three thousand portraits and scenes of Indian life, and penning voluminous notes in the form of letters—described how the buffalo often grazed on the lower parts of the prairie, where there was a little stagnant water lying among the grass:

> The ground underneath being saturated with it, is soft, into which the enormous bull, lowered down upon one knee, will plunge his horns, and at last his head, driving up the earth, and soon making an excavation in the ground, into which the water filters from among the grass, forming for him in a few moments, a cool and comfortable bath, into which he plunges . . . he then throws himself flat upon his side, and forcing

himself admirably round, with his horn and his huge hump on his shoulders presented to the sides, he ploughs up the ground by his rotary motion, sinking himself deeper and deeper into the ground, continually enlarging his pool, in which he at length becomes nearly immersed.

As many as a hundred bulls disporting, one after another, in a single wallow, produced a circular excavation 15 or 20 feet in diameter and a couple of feet deep, which soon filled with water. On the drier high prairies these "sinks," with which a square mile might be pockmarked, and into which water was constantly draining, served in the absence of springs as an invaluable drinking supply during droughts, but in the course of time they became choked with vegetable deposits, and the resulting humus encouraged an exceptionally rank growth, particularly of spear grass, around their edges. The conspicuous circles of these former wallows were a characteristic feature of buffalo country, outlasting even the famous buffalo trails.

The buffalo also regularly visited salt licks, congregating in thousands, according to Catlin, on the hundreds of acres of low-lying ground bordering the upper Missouri which, after the 3 or 4 feet of spring floodwaters had evaporated in the summer, were covered, as if with snow, by a rich deposit of salt.

During the rut, or the "running season" as it was known among the plainsmen, which fell in July, August, or September according to locality, the buffalo also assembled in such numbers as to "blacken" some parts of the prairies for miles. "It is no uncommon thing at this season, at these gatherings" [wrote Catlin] "to see several thousands in a mass, eddying and wheeling about under a cloud of dust, which is raised by the bulls as they are pawing in the dirt, or engaged in desperate combats . . . plunging and biting at each other in the most furious manner. . . . The males are continually following the females, and the whole mass are in constant motion; and all bellowing in deep and hollow sounds; which, mingled together, appear, at the distance of a mile or two, like the sound of distant thunder."

Except when concentrating at river crossings in the course of their migrations, the only other circumstances in which buffalo formed herds thousands strong was when stampeding. This they were likely to do when harassed by hunters, and frequently, for no apparent reason, running for 10 or 20 miles. And a stampede was the only occasion when the buffalo, thundering blindly en masse at 30 miles per hour, presented any danger to man. Indeed Dodge considered them the most harmless of animals, never doing more, even during the rutting and calving seasons, than demonstrating ferociously with tossing heads and pawing hooves or charge indecisively at a hunter, though if the latter continued to approach, the whole herd wheeled away and galloped off.

Although Dodge stated, inexplicably, that he had never witnessed a single instance of sustained combat between two bulls, and no action more aggressive than a clashing of horns, animosity between the bulls was not in fact restricted to the rutting season. Three days after Townsend had encountered immense numbers of buffalo on May 20, for example, all had disappeared from the Platte, and it was not until he had ridden some miles inland from the river to an extensive sandy plain that he saw great clouds of dust rising and circling in the air, and, on approaching nearer, came upon the buffalo rolling over and over in the sand with astonishing agility:

> Occasionally two of the bulls would spring from the ground and attack each other with amazing address and fury, retreating for ten or twelve feet, and then rushing suddenly forward, and dashing their enormous fronts together with a shock that seemed annihilating. In these recontres, one of the combat-

tants was often thrown upon his haunches, and tumbled sprawling upon the ground.

The immense numbers of buffalo grazing in a single locality necessitated a leisurely though continuous migration in search of fresh grazing, as one pasture after another was exhausted, and also frequent shorter treks to water, though they could survive without drinking for three days. The tracks, up to 12 inches deep and 16 inches broad, they trod out when converging on their traditional watering places from many miles out on the prairies were probably partly responsible for the widespread but erroneous belief among hunters and plainsmen that the legendary buffalo trails, which remained visible long after the buffalo had vanished from the plains, were engineered by the herds in the course of seasonal migrations extending for a thousand miles or more from one climatic zone to another—south in the autumn, north in the spring.

There is no reliable evidence that they undertook migratory movements comparable to those of, say, caribou, and J. A. Allen—the most reliable of contemporary buffalo historians, though he did not himself see the herds until 1871—pointed out that these trails were in fact limited in extent. The streams throughout the buffalo's range flowed mainly in an east and west direction, and the herds in passing constantly from the broad grassy divides, which they followed from one stream to another, trod out trails running at right angles to the general course of the streams, and therefore almost north and south.

The buffalo were nomadic rather than migratory, roaming over vast tracts of prairie, with a tendency to move north and south with the seasons. We know from Dodge that the movements of the southern herds were extremely erratic, influenced partly by weather conditions but primarily by the availability of grass; and he describes how early in the spring, as soon as the dry and desert-like prairie had begun to change from dingy brown to palest green, as the snow melted and the grass grew, the horizon would begin to be dotted with buffalo, singly or in groups of two or three:

> Thicker and thicker and in larger groups they come, until by the time the grass is well up the whole landscape appears a mass of buffalo, some individuals feeding, others standing, others lying down, but the herd moving slowly, moving constantly to the northward. . . .
>
> Some years . . . the buffalo appeared to move northward in one immense column, oftentimes from twenty to fifty miles in width, and of unknown depth from front to rear. Other years the same northward journey was made in several parallel columns, moving at the same rate, and with their numerous flankers covering a width of a hundred or more miles. . . .
>
> As the great herd proceeds northward it is constantly depleted, numbers wandering off to the right and left until finally it is scattered in small herds far and wide over the vast feeding-grounds where they pass the summer. . . . When the food in one locality fails they go to another, and towards fall, when the grass of the high prairie becomes parched by the heat and drought, they gradually work their way back to the South, concentrating on the rich grass of Texas and the Indian Territory (Oklahoma).

However, there is evidence that some of the most southerly herds might remain on their summer range throughout the winter, while the most northerly herds are reported to have retreated from the most exposed parts of the plains north of the Saskatchewan to shelter in the woods only during the heaviest snowfalls and most intense cold. Indeed, according to Catlin, the herds around Lake Winnipeg were able to find forage throughout the severest winter, mainly by "browsing amongst the timber, and by pawing through the snow, for a bite at the grass, which in those regions is frozen up very suddenly at the beginning of the winter, with all its juices in it, and consequently furnishes very nutritious and efficient food; and often, if not generally, supporting the animals in better flesh . . . than they are found to be in . . . upon the borders of Mexico, where the severity of winter is not known, but during a long . . . autumn, the herbage, under the influence of a burning sun, is gradually dried away to a mere husk."

According to Roe, there is no evidence that large numbers of buffalo were ever overwhelmed by snowstorms, for the northerly blizzards, associated with temperatures as low as 40 below zero, did not usually rage for longer than three days at a time, and while the snow might lie 3 or 4 feet deep on the plains, the winds swept the sides and tops of the hills clear, exposing the standing "hay." No doubt the herds often sought shelter in deep wooded ravines and canyons if these were within range, but they were capable of weathering a blizzard on the open prairie, sweeping away the snow from the cured grasses by swinging their massive, long-bearded heads from side to side, or shoving it aside with their muzzles, rather than scraping it away with their hooves. If the buffalo ever suffered heavy losses during snowstorms, it was probably when, in conditions similar to those prevailing with *djouts* on the steppes, both herbage and snow were frozen and they were unable to break through the ice crust. A widespread freeze-up may have been responsible for catastrophic losses on the Laramie plains in the winter of 1844–45 and again in 1876 when lack of forage was estimated to have resulted in the deaths of an improbable "several million" buffalo over 2500 square miles of the Brazos River prairies in Texas.

In the main, it was not severe winters that thinned the herds but prolonged summer droughts and, more regularly, the breakup of the river ice in the spring. Seton estimated that there were 20,000 miles of rivers on the buffalo range, and that these formed potential deathtraps for "hundreds of thousands" of buffalo every spring, because the herds were accustomed to cross frozen rivers by sliding across the ice in dense bunches, with the result that their concentrated mass weight was likely to break the ice if it was thin or rotten. Calves were also frequently drowned in these crossings because the cows were unable to help them up the steep-sided banks of the rivers.

Alexander Henry described how from March 28 to May 2 one year several thousand buffalo were drowned during the breakup of the ice on the Red River, and at one period the carcasses of entire herds were drifting downstream in one continuous line in the current for two days and nights. On May 18, 1795, John McDonnell counted the bodies of 7360 buffalo drowned or mired in quicksands on the Qu'Appelle River, and even during the rutting season in the late summer Catlin observed an instance of several meeting their death in quicksands when a great herd was crossing the Upper Missouri. He describes how, for a few hours, "The river was filled, and in parts blackened, with their heads and horns, as they were . . . making desperate battle while swimming. . . . From the immense numbers that had passed the river at that place, they had torn down the prairie bank of fifteen feet in height, so as to form a sort of road or landing place, where they all in succession clambered up."

Dodge also refers to the hazard of quicksands, recounting how:

Late in the summer of 1867 a herd of probably 4,000 buffalo attempted to cross the South Platte. . . . The water was rapidly subsiding, being nowhere over a foot in depth, and the channels in the bed were filled or filling with loose quicksands. The buffalo in front were soon hopelessly stuck. Those immediately behind, urged on by the horns and pressure of those yet farther in the rear, trampled on their struggling companions, to be themselves engulfed in the . . . sand . . . until the bed of the river, nearly half a mile broad, was covered with dead or dying buffalo. Only a comparatively few actually crossed the river. . . . . It was estimated that considerably over half the herd paid for this attempt with their lives.

Natural phenomena and natural predators never, however, threatened the survival of the buffalo, which appear to have been long-lived, for cows (with calves at foot) slaughtered in Wainwright Park, Alberta, in 1940 were reported to have been earmarked forty years earlier. Only man could ultimately exterminate their herds. Nevertheless, for thousands of years the Indians took only a very small toll of the buffalo, because they could only kill them in numbers when they were snowed up in ravines and helpless against the attacks of men on snowshoes, though they also herded them into ravines, or stampeded them over cliffs, or circled a herd on foot, slowly constricting the circle by running around the buffalo, whooping, until close enough to kill them with arrows and lances. Even after the Indians had learned to hunt the buffalo with the aid of the numerous pony mustangs, whose motley herds—colored milk-white, iron-gray, jet-black, skewbald, sorrel, and bay—ran wild on the plains and stampeded at sight of man a mile distant, they killed no more than could be replaced by the natural increase of the herds. But when in the 1830s the Indians were made aware of the white man's insatiable greed for meat and hides, their ruthless, incomparable horsemanship enabled them to slaughter the buffalo in immense numbers. Catlin cited one instance of a small band of Sioux slaughtering fourteen hundred buffalo in a few hours solely for the sake of their tongues which they traded for a gallon of whiskey. In the 1860s the new transcontinental railroads opened up the prairies to an endless ragtag and bobtail army of hide-hunters, commercial and military meat and tallow purveyors, indiscriminate pot-hunters, prospectors, and pioneers.

Although it was still possible in the autumn of 1868 for a train on the Kansas Pacific Railroad to travel for 120 miles through an almost unbroken aggregation of buffalo, and to be forced to halt time and again to allow large herds to cross the line, it was unusual a few years later to see more than a few herds of ten or twenty beasts, for by 1870, after a massacre of the herds on an unprecedented scale by the Sioux in order to obtain hides for trading, the buffalo's original habitat had been split in two, with the southern "herd" ranging from northern Texas to about 41°30′N, and the northern "herd" from about 43°N into Canada. The further slaughter of possibly four and a half million buffalo of the southern herd in the three years 1872–74 presaged the doom of the prairie's most magnificent inhabitant. By 1888 the herds had been decimated almost to the last beast, and by the end of the century only about 750 survived in all America. That this nucleus has been able to increase under protection to its present strength of about 50,000 in various reserves is a near miracle for which the American people in general can take no credit.

The buffalo shared the prairies with almost as many million pronghorn antelope—forty million was Seton's informed guess—though by 1908 their numbers too had been reduced to less than twenty thousand north of Mexico, but have since recovered to about one-third of a million. With a hundred million fewer herbivores at work on the grass, trees were able to infiltrate the plains here and there, and mule and black-tailed deer have colonized them from the peripheral woodlands. Because the numbers of buffalo and pronghorns were so great, they cannot have conflicted significantly for forage on the same range,

Pronghorn antelope

and though the pronghorns grazed over the higher, drier prairies in the summer, taking some grass, we know that they fed mainly on shrubs and plants that competed with grasses. The gray-green sagebrush, which grew in extensive stands on the gravelly uplands, was particularly sought after, and the pronghorns also ate plants that were poisonous to domestic stock and presumably to the buffalo. In the winter they cleaned up the stalks of coarser grasses neglected by the buffalo though, again, foraging mainly on shrubby plants on hillsides and ridges swept clear of snow by the winds.

When summer droughts forced the buffalo to migrate in search of water and fresh pasture, the pronghorns, which tolerated temperatures of 100° F, and also those well below zero, could still obtain both food and water from the prickly pear and other cacti whose spines were young and soft or set far enough apart to allow them to poke their narrow muzzles between them. Even when fires swept over the plains, the prickly pear usually survived with its fleshy fruit intact, suffering no greater harm than singed spines. Indeed it actually flourished during droughts, possibly benefiting from lack of competition by less resistant plants, for its root systems, extending horizontally for many yards in every direction an inch or two below the surface, absorbed any surface moisture, while its branches or joints stored and held immense quantities of water. At the end of a two- or three-year drought, almost the only green plants on the plains were those of the prickly pear.

It was during a three-week period in the late summer that the pronghorn bucks rounded up harems of from seven to exceptionally fifteen does, and at the conclusion of the rut and with the first heavy falls of snow migrated in herds of a hundred or more southward for 100 or 150 miles from northern habitats, though remaining on their summer pastures in regions where the winters were mild and snowfall light. From late April to mid-June, according to locality, the herds broke up and the does scattered in twos or threes to drop their fawns—one in the case of a young doe, two subsequently—in the cover of long grass.

The pronghorn's fleetness of foot and endurance were superior to those of any other prairie animal. Within a couple of weeks of birth the fawns could exceed 25 miles per hour, but although J. A. Allen credited the adults with the ability to gallop in near 20-foot bounds at 60 miles per hour for three or four minutes, it was Dodge's experience that they could be run down by an exceptionally fast greyhound, and it is generally held that a speed of 40 miles per hour with sporadic bursts of up to 45 miles per hour is a more realistic estimate. The pronghorns were therefore probably little faster than coyotes with a top speed of 40 miles per hour or wolves with one of 45 miles per hour, but they could run for 15 miles at a stretch without resting, and for half that distance never drop below 30 or 35 miles per hour, and only infrequently below 40 miles per hour.

Moreover, when pursued by wolves or coyotes, they tended to run a straight course—unlike most true antelopes and gazelles—thereby preventing predators, when hunting in packs, from shortening the chase by cutting corners, or from relaying one another as coyotes were reputed to do. Although, according to Dodge, a solitary buck would fight off a wolf, and a herd of pronghorns display no fear of a pack of wolves, they were so well equipped defensively as to suggest that predators, presumably mainly wolves, must have been extremely numerous. They were swift of foot; they had unusually large and prominent eyes, set well to the side of the face and covering a wide field of view without head movement; they had acute senses of hearing and smell, and were ever on the alert, raising their heads every few seconds when grazing; and they possessed a simple but effective herd-warning apparatus. Victor H. Cahalane has described in *Mammals of North America* the pronghorn's reaction to danger:

At the first appearance of danger anywhere on the horizon, the antelope throws up its head and stares. The great black eyes dilate, the pointed ears, five inches high and three inches broad, are thrown forward to scoop in the faintest sound. For an instant the beautifully marked body is tense. At the same moment, the twin white discs on the buttocks serve as heliographs. The alarm causes a contraction of special muscles, and the multitude of white hairs at the rear rise instantly. These flaring patches reflect an astonishing amount of light. Other antelope may see these signals a couple of miles away. They immediately repeat it, and the warning is then spread far and wide. Even fawns a few hours old erect their rosettes, although theirs are dulled by a tinge of brown. The whole plains landscape seems to be dotted with flying rump patches.

Simultaneously, as the rump signal is flashed, a strong musky scent is released from a set of twin glands located in the muscles that erect the glistening hairs. . . .

As soon as the members of a band see and smell the warning signals and repeat them for the benefit of others, they dash to a rallying point. Then the bands act as one unit, galloping, wheeling, and stopping to look back as if on command.

5: White Wolves and Gray

Although the plains grizzlies are known to have killed buffalo, one presumes that they did so infrequently, and that the buffalo's only major predator was the wolf. The very large buffalo wolves—some so pale in color as to appear white at a distance— were formerly extremely numerous on the prairies; but they had been totally exterminated before the end of the nineteenth century, just as the gray timber wolves had been almost wiped out in the United States south of the 50th parallel by 1935, with the result that today only the Superior National Forest in northern Minnesota holds any sizable population of wolves (between three hundred and seven hundred), though there are still upward of twenty-five thousand in Alaska and about the same number in Canada.

Surprisingly little information is available about the buffalo wolves. It is generally believed that calving buffalo cows, which were only half the weight of the bulls, young beasts, which accompanied their mothers until four years old, and old bulls, wandering alone without herd protection, were heavily preyed on by wolves. Seton, however, states that they did not kill large numbers, and Dodge describes them as extremely timid—the most harmless to beasts and least dangerous to man of all carnivores—with a single wolf not venturing to attack a sheep, and a pack only occasionally a solitary ox or cow. But Dodge and his contemporaries were describing conditions in which the prairie wolves were primarily scavengers in "gangs" of as many as fifty or sixty, obtaining the bulk of their food from the immense numbers of buffalo carcasses left rotting on the plains by Indians and whites alike, and preying only on the sick and the old. But even before the massacre of the herds had begun, Captain William Clark of the 1804–6 Lewis and Clark expedition from the Missouri to the Columbia noted that: "I observe, near all large gangues of Buffalow, wolves, and when the Buffalow move these animals follow, and feed on those that are killed by accident or those that are too pore or fat to keep up with the gangue."

And Catlin also describes how:

Whilst the herd is together, the wolves never attack them, as they instantly gather for combined resistance. . . . But when the herds are travelling, it often happens that an aged or wounded one lingers at a distance behind, and when fairly out of sight of the herd, is set upon by these voracious hunters, which often gather to the number of fifty or more, and are sure at last to torture him to death. . . . But a short time since . . . we discovered a huge bull encircled with a gang of white wolves . . . the animal had made desperate resistance, until his eyes were entirely eaten out of his head—the grizzle of his nose was mostly gone—his tongue was half eaten off, and the skin and flesh of his legs torn almost literally into strings.

There is, or was until very recently, an unsubstantiated theory among some zoologists that large carnivores prey mainly on animals in the prime of life. But, as L. David Mech has shown in his study of gray wolves, the latter prey largely on the sick, the old, and the young—primarily those less than one year old or those that have lived at least half their probable life-span in the wild state—and it is not likely that any pack of buffalo wolves would have tackled the prime bulls when they formed up in defense of the cows and calves.

The gray wolves, unlike the buffalo wolves, have been patiently and in some cases sympathetically studied by a number of naturalists. A pack usually consists of from two to eight individuals, no doubt related and centered around a breeding pair, and led by one wolf who initiates a hunt by waking up the others. Packs of as many as thirty-six have, however, been reliably reported, and the strength of a pack will be determined, as Mech has pointed out, by such factors as the smallest unit required to locate and bring down prey efficiently and, complementary to this, the largest number for which a kill will provide sufficient food. A 150-pound deer would not, for example, satisfy a pack of sixty wolves.

Pack size and the incidence of prey will also determine the hunting range. The winter range of a dog and a bitch may cover only 36 square miles, whereas that of a pack of ten may extend over 5000 square miles or more. Although hunting packs are known to average 14 or 15 miles a day on the trail, even under difficult winter conditions, the actual distance covered during the pursuit of prey probably rarely exceeds 5 miles, for contrary to the popular belief that wolves wear down their prey by loping tirelessly after them mile upon mile, they in fact—like so many other carnivores—rely mainly on a stalk, a quick burst of speed in 16-foot bounds, and a short chase to bring down their victim, seldom exceeding a speed of 25 miles per hour for more than 1 or 2 miles at a time, though capable of 35 to 45 miles per hour.

According to Lois Crisler, even a caribou calf can run faster than a wolf. Normally a pursuit is broken off after twenty minutes if unsuccessful, and a ten-minute rest taken before the pack sets off in search of other prey. Wolves are quick to spot any moving object, and can also scent game when 300 yards and, under certain conditions, 1½ miles downwind of them. Nevertheless, a pack's chances of making a successful kill are perhaps no better than one in ten, and after a night's hunting a wolf may be so exhausted that in Adolph Murie's words in *A Naturalist in Alaska*, "When he arrives at the den, he flops, relaxes completely, and may not even change his position for three to four hours. Often he may not even raise his head to look around for intruders."

By the end of a day's hunting the pack may indeed have traveled 20 miles from its home base, and a male may have carried a load of meat, bolted whole, in his stomach all that way back to the den to disgorge to a litter of cubs and sometimes to the bitch or to another member of the pack who has remained on guard while the pack is away hunting, for the cubs, which are born in mid-May, remain in the den for the first three weeks of their lives, and do not hunt with the pack until the late autumn. Indeed, since they have to be taught how to hunt, they run with their parents for almost a year.

A wild wolf's sense of social responsibility is comparable to that of the elephant. As Lois Crisler has pointed out in her beautiful book, *Arctic Wild*, both male and female wolves will care for and feed cubs that are not their own; a wolf will whimper in sympathy with its dog companion when the latter cries out from the pain of porcupine quills in its nose, or remain to keep company with a chained whimpering dog. Unlike Konrad Lorenz's

Homo sapiens, with his latent terrible drives of a very irascible ape, wolves are nonaggressive and, in Captain Meriwether Lewis' words more than 170 years ago, "extremely gentle," fighting among themselves only under great stress and becoming most upset if dog companions fight. Mech has suggested that another factor controlling pack size may be the maximum number of other wolves with which an individual can form social bonds or, alternatively, the degree of social competition it can accept. One of the wolves' social bonds is their community howling, though no doubt this also serves to assemble the pack when its members have become separated in the course of a hunt, as often happens, and it also advertises the pack's presence in their hunting territory over an area of as much as 50 square miles. "Mountain men in the old West," says Lois Crisler, "gathered valuable clues about movements of Indians and wild animals from the changeful voices of the wolves."

Nevertheless, community howling, which may take place by day as often as by night, and probably at any season of the year, and may be answered by neighboring packs 4 miles or more distant, is, as Lois Crisler observed, a happy occasion:

> Wolves love a howl. When it is started they instantly seek contact with one another, troop together, fur to fur. Some wolves . . . will run from any distance, panting and bright-eyed, to join in, uttering, as they run, fervent little wows, jaws wide, hardly able to wait to sing. . . .
> One wolf begins, and after its first or second howl others join in. Each animal starts more or less by itself, beginning with a few long, low howls and working up to a series of shorter, higher ones, somewhat in chorus with those of other pack members. Such a session lasts an average of eighty-five seconds and is sometimes followed by a repeat performance. . . . The wolves would break off suddenly and there would be a listening silence. . . . After a pack once ends its howling

sessions, there appears to be a period of fifteen to twenty minutes or more during which the animals will not or cannot
howl. . . .

There are many howls—the happy social howl, the mourning howl, the wild deep hunting howl . . . strange, savage,
heart-stirring. . . . All are beautiful. The wolf's voice is pure
except when the wolf is crushed by despair.

One wolf may howl by itself—a long, low, mournful moan
lasting for an average of thirty-five seconds and repeated several
times, as Lois Crisler describes:

> Sometimes she ululated, drawing her tongue up and down
> in her mouth like a trombone slide. Sometimes on a long note
> she held the tip of her tongue curled against the roof of her
> mouth. She shaped her notes with her cheeks, retracting them
> for plangency, or holding the sound in with them for horn
> notes. She must have had pleasure and sensitiveness about her
> song for if I entered [howled] on her note she instantly shifted
> by a note or two; wolves avoid unison singing; they like
> chords. . . . Few humans now have ever heard the howl of a
> wolf and that only the captive howl, like the howling of the
> slave dogs of the North.

Now that the wolves are gone from the plains, the voice of the
prairie between sunset and sunrise is that of the coyotes, whose
shrill, staccato, yelping barks, slurred together into a long, qua-
vering, wild cry, terminate in a series of earsplitting howls.
They too sometimes pack to "sing" in mournful medley, though
"each in its own orchestration," in Cahalane's words, "with an
astounding chorus of whines, barks, howls and wails ranging
across at least two full octaves . . . that seem to rise all the way
to the stars and beyond."

During the past hundred years these very successful "prairie
wolves"—only one-half or one-third the size of the gray wolves
and resembling a cross between fox and wolf, with their long

narrow muzzles, large pointed ears, slender legs, small feet, and bushy tails—have invaded the central prairies, despite persecution by poisoning, trapping, and hunting as intensive, unrelenting, and merciless as that which exterminated the wolves. A score of races now range throughout the United States from diminutives in the Southwestern deserts to the largest in the montane forests and even above the timberline, and for 7500

The coyote or "prairie wolf"

miles from Mexico and Costa Rica to northern Alaska. For that matter they have, like English foxes, also infiltrated large towns, subsisting, undetected by most city dwellers, on mice and insects, scraps and garbage.

Why have the coyotes succeeded where the wolves failed? It is partly perhaps because they have always been able to replace their losses, for although an average litter contains five or six pups, as many as nineteen have been recorded; partly because of their small size, coupled with their foxlike ability to live undetected in the midst of men and therefore to be familiar with the habits of man; but mainly because they have been able to adapt to every kind of environment and subsist on every kind of food from the fawns of antelope and mule deer to hares, rabbits, chipmunks, mice, and carrion, together with quail and other ground-nesting birds, and an unlimited range of vegetable foods, including grass, nuts, juniper berries, rose hips, peaches, apricots, pears, plums, grapes, cherries, watermelons, and particularly the juicy fruits of the prickly pear and the beans of the mesquite.

When hunting an adult deer they usually do so in pairs—though sometimes in packs—with one stampeding the prey toward the other, but even a single coyote is capable of killing a 200-pound buck. A pair will also cooperate in killing a porcupine, after pawing it over onto its back, with one tugging at a foreleg and the other at a hind leg. In this way the porcupine's slashing spined tail is rendered inoperative, while its unprotected belly is vulnerable. By contrast, although badgers have been known to dig out coyote pups and eat them, a number of instances have been recorded of curious friendships between some coyotes and badgers. One old-timer in Wyoming described seeing a coyote and a badger walking together: "The coyote would go in front of the badger, lay its head on the latter's neck, lick it, jump into the air, and give other expressions of unmistakable joy . . . the badger seemed equally pleased."

Coyotes enjoy the further advantage over wolves of not requiring to drink regularly except in very hot weather, though those living in desert regions are able to scent water lying below the surface of dry washes or arroyos and they dig sloping tunnels 4 or 5 feet down to this; nor do the pups need water for the first few months, and their den may be half a dozen miles from the nearest water. Denning sites present no problem, since these are usually the earths of other animals such as porcupines or badgers or the enlarged burrows of prairie dogs or rabbits, and the bitch may clean out a dozen dens and move the pups from one to another if disturbed. For the first month or six weeks the male brings food to his mate, some of which she disgorges to the pups, but after eight or ten weeks the den is abandoned, though the pups remain with their parents until the early autumn.

6: Gophers and Prairie Dogs

The nomadic buffalo and pronghorns were not, ecologically, the most important inhabitants of the prairies. As on the steppes, so on the prairies it was the rodents—the voles, gophers, and ground squirrels that were the most influential. The prairie climate varies, like that of the steppes, from extreme heat in the summer to extreme cold in the winter, and is also subject to sudden violent storms. Buffalo and antelope could weather these extremes or escape them by migrating, but the smaller sedentary mammals' only refuge was their burrows. For thousands of years those small ground squirrels, the famous prairie dogs, had deep-plowed the prairies, tilling, cultivating, and aerating them with their incessant burrowing, had fertilized them with their droppings and deposits of vegetation, irrigated them with the depressions between the mounds of spoil they excavated, mowed them—98 percent of their food was grass—and weeded them by eating any herbs intruding among the grasses, cutting down every plant more than 6 inches high within 75 to 100 feet of their burrows. Indeed, they sited their townships in areas where heavy grazing by the buffalo had thinned out the taller grasses, thereby creating open ground commanding a field of view against predators, while the short blue grama and buffalo grasses, which largely replaced the tall grasses in such conditions, provided good grazing for the pronghorns.

Complementary to the prairie dogs were the almost exclusively subterranean pocket gophers, of which there were some three hundred varieties. These inhabited the bushy and wooded parts of the plains, where there were no townships of prairie dogs, and, subsisting on bulbs and roots absent in grassy areas, maintained and perhaps increased the area of grassland by constantly cutting beneath woody vegetation and eliminating this wherever it extended into the prairie. Though nongregarious, and fighting fiercely when meeting, except when the males roamed across country in search of the equally solitary females during the mating season, the solitary pocket gophers threw up, like moles, countless small mounds of spoil from their tunnelings in search of food, which they transported to their subterranean storerooms in their enormous cheek pouches, fur-lined like those of kangaroo rats and spiny and pocket mice. Cahalane has described how a pocket gopher, working with both hands so swiftly that the human eye can hardly follow them, inserts food or nest material first into one pouch and then into the other: long flexible pieces of grass and thin roots being crammed farther and farther back into the pouches, while unwieldy clumps of food may either be eaten on the spot, or dragged to the burrow, or cut up into 2- or 3-inch fragments and stuffed into the pouches.

A single gopher was capable of excavating 200 or 300 feet of tunnel in one night, and a tunnel system of deep runways from

1½ to 3 inches in diameter, constructed and inhabited by only one gopher, might be half a mile long:

> The spur shaft of each entrance [writes Cahalane] slants down and opens into the intricate maze of feeding galleries . . . six inches or as much as three feet below the surface. . . . At several points, little rooms are located just off the travel route or at the end of spur tunnels. These are the upper store rooms. Some contain the remains of food left over from the previous winter; others are filled with freshly gathered supplies. There may be as many as eight or ten rooms. Stocks containing 2,300 grass cuttings and 175 bulbs have been found in one cache alone . . . it always brings home more than it can eat. The result is that much of the food spoils. Some of the old galleries are packed solidly with all sorts of refuse.

Though now reduced by a massive poisoning campaign and the destruction of their habitat to remnant populations, the prairie dogs, and in particular the black-tailed species—the barking squirrel or *petit chien*—were formerly numbered in millions. A density of twenty-five burrows to the acre was common, and three or four times that concentration possible. In 1900 it was estimated that one aggregation of townships in Texas extended over an area of 25,000 square miles, and that their four hundred million inhabitants—an informed guess allowing for the many unoccupied burrows—were consuming grass sufficient for one and a half million cattle. Reputedly, thousands of similar-sized aggregations existed in the eastern parts of New Mexico, in Colorado, Wyoming, and Montana, in the western parts of Oklahoma, and in Nebraska and South Dakota west of the Missouri.

The prairie dogs' distribution appears to have been influenced by climatic factors. Their strongholds were the sunny arid plains of the West, despite the fact that in these regions they might have to survive without water for periods of years when the rains failed, and as the dry plains gave way eastward to the damp, more luxuriantly vegetated prairies of the Mississippi Valley, so their townships became less and less numerous. Yet according to C. Hart Merriam, who was studying prairie dogs in the early years of this century, they thrived on the rich vegetation of irrigated areas of the Western plains. Although they neither stored food nor hibernated, they put on an immense amount of fat during the summer and were indeed almost obese by the autumn when they came less aboveground, and they were able to remain belowground, subsisting on this reserve of fat, for long periods during heavy falls of snow in the more northerly parts of their range. Nevertheless they were aboveground almost every winter's day in more southerly latitudes, while their cousins, the white-tailed prairie dogs of the northern Rockies, would even venture out onto the snow after subzero night temperatures, providing that the sun was shining.

The colossal aggregations of prairie dogs were split up into distinct communities or "towns," completely isolated one from another by such natural barriers as rivers, hills, and ridges, and the total absence of any intercourse between towns must have contributed to their extermination. If, for example, all but a dozen dogs were poisoned in one town, then that community was doomed to extinction because the burrows of the survivors were too widely scattered for their occupants to warn each other against predators, while there were not enough dogs to cut down the plants and tall grasses, whose removal provided the essential cleared ground. With the virtual extinction of the prairie dogs, and of the buffalo and pronghorns, the prairies were invaded and colonized by alien plants, especially thistles, woody shrubs, and mesquites.

The larger towns were further separated into "wards" by differences in terrain or vegetation, though there was some interchange of inhabitants between these, and also vocal communication, in the form of a variety of chirps and sharp doglike barks, which warned all the members of the ward of the presence of a predator. When the alarm was sounded, there was a rush of feeding dogs to the mounds at the entrance to their burrows, and on these they would sit or stand erect, twitching their tails and chattering or barking, before plunging headlong into the funnel-shaped entrances and then perhaps turning around and popping their heads above the crater-shaped rims of the mounds. Costello has described in *The Prairie World* how when a man approached a colony: "The prairie dogs one hundred yards or more ahead sit erect and chirp at a moderate rate. As you approach, the tempo of chirping increases, the dogs drop to their bellies on top of their crater mounds. At fifty to one hundred feet, just when they seem ready to explode with chirping they dive below."

Within the wards there were also closed social, basically family groups known as "coteries" or "clans." These consisted of from two to thirty members—typically a male, three females, and six young ones—which either shared an elaborate communal burrow system or occupied individual burrows, but moved freely within the coterie's territorial limits and shared in its corporate activities. There was much visiting of neighbors' burrows, associated with kiss greetings with bared teeth, though from time to time the owner of a burrow would demonstrate its territorial rights by rearing up on its hind legs and, throwing its head violently up and backward, crying *whee-ool*, before dropping down on all fours again. Dogs running for cover from a predator into other dogs' burrows were summarily ejected.

According to Costello the prairie dogs would begin to emerge from their burrows soon after sunrise on clear summer days. After basking for a while, "breakfast" might occupy them for two or three hours, since the meal would be interrupted by many pauses to watch for enemies, to greet near neighbors, or to chase away intruders. During the heat of the day they rested in their burrows, resuming their activities in the afternoon until sundown.

The advantages of the coterie's social organization were that the maximum number of young could be reared because the members of a coterie were not antagonistic; while on the other hand the defense of one coterie's territory against individuals of another precluded overpopulation by invasion from outside and guaranteed an equable distribution of grazing land. However, once the young dogs were independent of their parents, the latter moved home to the periphery of the coterie, thus extending its limits, though according to Merriam the majority of the young were quickly killed off by predators.

Burrow entrances were normally 50 feet or more apart, though in densely populated towns this distance might be reduced to 30 or even 10 feet. In such circumstances the bare dusty places between the burrows provided the buffalo with favorite rolling places, for Merriam has described how:

> The ground immediately surrounding each burrow is usually cleared of small plants and kept clean and bare, and where burrows are near together the bare areas often join, so that in thickly populated colonies the ground is hard and smooth . . . and the animals are obliged to go some distance for food. This they dislike, lest they be pounced upon by enemies; hence, when the grass near their burrows has been consumed they dig new holes nearer the supply. It takes a long time for vegetation to regain a foothold on the hard floors of the dog towns, and the sites of old towns remain conspicuous for years after they are abandoned.

Prairie dogs—typical greeting

Merriam and others have sketched the plan of the tubelike burrow, which varied from 4½ inches to 6 or 8 inches in diameter, and was usually dug at a steep angle to depths varying between 3 and 14½ feet, before turning almost at right angles and continuing horizontally for as much as 13½ feet. A short lateral tunnel from the horizontal one led to the nest, lined with dried grasses or shredded plant stems, while from 3 to 5 feet below the entrance another short side tunnel, with space for one dog only, served as a kind of guardroom, from which the owner could bark at an intruder or in which it could stay for a while, before returning cautiously to the mouth of the burrow.

The entrance to the burrow was surrounded by the elevated mound of excavated spoil 1 or 2 feet high and 3 or 4 in diameter—though as much as 10 feet if the burrow had been occupied for a long time—tamped and molded by the occupants' paws and blunt noses, and repaired when breached by heavy rain. Although these mounds served as lookouts for their occupants which, with their slightly rounded heads and high-set eyes, could peer over the rim of the crater with only a small portion of the head exposed, their primary function was to prevent the burrows from being flooded during heavy rainstorms.

Moreover, as Merriam pointed out, there were occasions when the mounds were not sufficiently high to prevent the inrush of water on irrigated lands or during sudden downpours, and the prairie dogs provided a unique avenue of escape for use when they were threatened with drowning. Shallow burrows, with laterals not deeper than 3½ feet below the ground level, were provided with additional laterals which reached to within 6 inches of the surface. As the water inundated the burrow, the rodents repaired to these ascending levels, where they could remain in comparative safety for several hours or longer, for the inrush of water caused an air pocket to form in the top of the lateral which lasted until the air could escape through the earth. This appeared to be the most logical explanation of why few prairie dogs were drowned even though known to have been completely underwater for several hours at different times during the season.

Despite their deep burrows and mound defenses, the prairie dogs were heavily preyed on, and when the ranchers began to exterminate the predators, and also to improve the grazing for their herds, their numbers initially multiplied dramatically. Their enemies included wolves, coyotes, bobcats, badgers, and weasels, raptors such as eagles and prairie hawks, and also snakes, especially rattlesnakes which have always been extremely numerous and widely distributed over the prairies.

Rattlesnakes, which entered occupied burrows to shelter from the sun and to hibernate in the winter, supplemented their diet of mice, kangaroo rats, lizards, and salamanders with the young of the prairie dogs and of the burrowing owls, though contrary to popular belief, the latter occupied only abandoned burrows, as did hibernating box turtles and large toads. Prairie hawks, which were formerly very common on the plains, specialized in hunting prairie dogs, profiting by the fact that, though the latter were extremely alert, they never looked upward for danger. Coyotes would stalk up to a township when the prairie dogs were underground, wait until they had come out to feed, and then cut one off from its burrow. The powerful badgers either scented out occupied burrows and dug down to the inmates or frightened the prairie dogs into their burrows and then dug them out. Weasels were lean enough to pursue the dogs into their burrows and move freely through the tunnels. Indeed the black-footed ferrets—the North American form of the Old World polecat—which lived in unoccupied burrows in the townships, were so dependent on the prairie dogs as a source of food that, with their extermination and also as a result of feeding on poisoned corpses and on poisoned meat laid out for coyotes, they have become one of the rarest of the prairie mammals, surviving perhaps only in Alberta and South Dakota, where they suffer further losses from trigger-happy gunners and traffic on the highways.

7: Survival in
   North American Deserts

In the deserts of the American Southwest and Mexico, the prairie dogs are replaced by other, miniature ground squirrels, not much more than 6 inches long including tails. According to Knut Schmidt-Nielsen these squirrels remain in their burrows during the hottest hours at midsummer, since they cannot tolerate the direct heat of the midday sun, and are active mainly in the early morning and late afternoon, when they dash about from one place to another, though mainly in the shade, frequently disappearing into their small burrows in the sand under bushes, only to pop out again a few seconds later to chase insects, nibble at green leaves, or dig scrapes. Like the susliks of Asian deserts they have to adapt to extremes of temperature ranging from 15° F at night to 134° F at noon, when the ground temperature may exceed 160° F, reaching 190° F in July 1958 at Tule Spring in Death Valley, California.

If a steppe can be described as a place where eggs fry and

mercury freezes, this is even truer of a desert, where the temperature of the soil just below the surface may vary by more than 100° F in twenty-four hours. However, one species, the antelope ground squirrel—better known perhaps as the desert chipmunk—has developed such resistance to a high body temperature that it may be active throughout the day, catching the beetles, grasshoppers, and crickets that form 90 percent of its food during the summer and autumn, supplemented by the fruits of cacti and Joshua trees, retreating into shade or into its burrow only when its temperature reaches a critical level. Though traveling considerable distances to drink when water is available, it can survive for months without it, and though subsisting on underground stores of seeds during the barren desert winter, does not hibernate, whereas the ground squirrels of the Mojave Desert not only hibernate in the winter, but also aestivate from late August or early September through the hottest months of the dry autumn, thereby economizing in their water requirements. Similarly, the round-tailed ground squirrels inhabiting the flat silt valleys in the Arizona desert, in which there is very little shade and only sufficient fresh grass, roots, and mesquite leaves (from which they also obtain liquid) for short periods, are obliged to hibernate for a total of eight months every year in their relatively cool burrows, wherein the temperature never rises above 80° F even when that of the surface soil is heated to its maximum.

It is the summer rains, responsible for flash floods and filling water holes, that make it possible for the Arizona desert to contain one of the world's largest populations of toads, ranging from inch-long diminutives to giants that prey on tarantulas and half-grown quail. One does not normally associate amphibians with arid places, for not only must their skin be moist for respiration—frogs, for example, breathe largely through the skin and moist tissues of the mouth, and only partly with their lungs—but they are also dependent on surface water for the hatching of their eggs; but as we shall see in subsequent chapters, the presence of amphibians in a desert is by no means unique. During the eight or nine months of drought the toads, like the ground squirrels, hibernate; but when the rains eventually come, the hatching and development periods of the tadpoles are speeded up to anticipate the evaporation of the temporary pools in which the spawn was deposited. Thus the small spadefoot toad's eggs hatch within forty-eight hours, and the tadpoles develop legs for land use within twelve to fifteen days, by which time they are fully equipped to feed and to go into hibernation when the last of the pools has dried up.

But the fauna of American deserts would be drastically reduced were there no cacti and euphorbias which, encased in an impermeable leathery tissue, strengthened in some instances by wax, retain, like the prickly pear, quantities of water that enable them to survive four years or more of total drought. There are some sixteen hundred species of cacti, blooming for perhaps a single day once a year, and nowhere is there a greater variety than in the Sonoran desert. Almost every desert animal—the round-tailed squirrel is an exception—relies on cacti for food or moisture or shade, or all of these. Cactus-joint bugs, protected by their spines, feed on their juices; some fifty species of birds eat their fruits; peccaries dig up and chew their moisture-holding roots; and pack rats romp about even among the most densely spined cacti, and burrow at the base of the cholla cactus, whose roots radiate in networks 30 feet in diameter just below the surface, unlike the taproots of mesquite trees that penetrate 100 feet down into the sand dunes, and whose seeds, incidentally, are capable of germinating after lying dormant for forty-five years.

Pack rats, which resemble the common brown rat in size but have soft gray fur, white underparts, and furry tails, are crepuscular and nocturnal, and are famed for their mania for collecting objects when rustling around a camp at night. Metal ones that shine or glitter, such as coins, belt buckles, or keys, are preferred, though small stones, fragments of harness, animal droppings, tallow candles, and even sticks of dynamite are all on record. Frequently a pebble or other valueless object is left in place of the one appropriated, and this habit of making an exchange earned the animal the name of trade or pack rat among the old prospectors in the West, where there were fabulous legends of rats leaving solid nuggets of gold in payment for a cake of soap or other insignificant item.

As Schmidt-Nielsen has pointed out in *Desert Animals*, the joints of the cholla cactus are very easily detached, and the slightest brush against the plant results in a joint coming off and sticking painfully to one's skin. Hence its popular name, "jumping cholla," because its joints seem to grasp at the passerby. Although the spines are sharp enough to penetrate a leather boot if a detached joint is carelessly kicked, the pack rats climb agilely about the chollas, run over joints lying on the ground, and drag spiny portions to their nests—unharmed according to Schmidt-Nielsen, though Cahalane states that a rat may in fact injure or impale itself on the recurved spines when escaping from a predator. Where the cholla are numerous, the fleshy joints provide the rats with 50 percent of their food, additional to fresh grass and the green leaves and pods of mesquite (from which they too obtain moisture). Schmidt-Nielsen observed that they handled the joints "with great skill and deftness, biting only into the flesh between the spines without getting hurt, seemingly protected by an invisible armour."

In an arid environment the pack rats' living quarters consist of

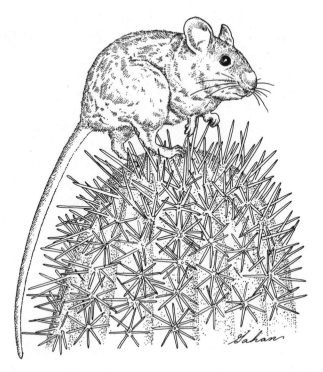

Pack rat on cholla cactus

a burrow under a heap of dead twigs and green vegetation mixed with dry dung, curios they may have collected, and other debris, particularly the spiny joints of the cholla, constructed in layers so that the twigs allow cooling air to circulate around the damp vegetable matter. A couple of feet high and several yards across, this superstructure shelters and protects the nest beneath, and is usually placed beside the trunk of a mesquite bush or cactus, whose partial shade lowers the temperature of the nest almost 50 percent below that of the open desert. The sharp spines of the cholla buds, through whose maze the rats have their special runways, protect the nest from some soft-skinned predators such as coyotes, though the slender cacomistle or ringtail penetrates the "boma" with ease, either to prey on the rats or to rear its young in a deserted nest. Mice, three species of skunks, and raccoons are also apparently impervious to the spines, while various armored snakes and lizards retreat to the cool heaps on hot days and also prey on the rats, and rattlesnakes hibernate in them during the winter, secure from predators.

The giant cactus wren also builds its round nest, with domed roof and narrow entrance tunnel, in the jumping-cholla's spines. Like other wrens it builds a number of nests and, by constantly switching from one to another, possibly confuses predators; while, if a rattlesnake penetrates the cactus, the harsh alarm notes of one wren attract a score of others, whose numbers and rapid movements render it difficult for the snake to strike at any one individual.

The largest of the cacti is the saguaro or giant cactus, whose cylindrical, fluted, and spiny columns, which may be simple or branched, reach a height of 30 or 50 feet. The saguaro is unique. According to a desert botanist, Volney M. Spaulding (quoted by Edmund C. Jaeger in *The North American Deserts*), it is:

Mechanically speaking, a huge reservoir of water, subjected to the stress of high winds, and so constructed that for a long period of years it not only maintains securely its erect position and steadily continues its growth but also promptly expands whenever the soil is wet, even for a short time. The construction of such a tank represents an engineering feat which probably has no parallel in any artificial structure in existence, and the case appears still more remarkable when it is considered that the whole system of storage in an adjustable tank is dependent for its highest efficiency on the peculiarities of its root system.

The saguaro's root system comprises a strong anchoring tap-root and thick secondary lateral roots, in addition to numerous, very long, superficial rootlets that serve mainly as moisture ab-sorbers. During the winter rains in the deserts of California and Arizona, not only do the long roots take in water, but also dry-season indentations or grooves in the trunks swell and oc-casionally split. When the saguaro is swollen with this reservoir of water, states Lewis Wayne Walker in an article in *Animals*, any bruise or cut can result in copious bleeding, though after the moisture has been stored for several weeks, it tends to thicken and eventually form a scab protecting any injury. Gilded flicker and gila woodpeckers probe the leathery-skinned columns for in-sects and, when they are swollen, excavate nesting holes, first drilling horizontally into the trunk for 6 or 8 inches and then downward perpendicularly for a further 14 inches or so. After hacking out a bulbous chamber at the bottom, they line this with dried saguaro which is waterproof, for although, according to Walker again, "while they are at work, and for days af-terwards, the ton or so of plant towering above drips moisture into this new cavity, and some settles on the bottom, most of it solidifies in contact with the air, forming a hard internal shell of scar-tissue."

When the young woodpeckers hatch, they benefit from the more constant temperature prevailing within their holes, which may be 20 degrees cooler on very hot days and 20 degrees warmer on cold nights, than those without; though because the holes are watertight, they can prove deathtraps in years of un-seasonable rains, when pools of water several inches deep collect in them, chilling eggs and drowning nestlings.

It is the woodpeckers' annual excavations that have made it possible for several other species of birds, and also bees, to colonize large areas of desert in which cacti are the only sizable vegetation. Ash-throated flycatchers, elf owls, screech owls, American sparrow hawks, and whippoorwills will take advantage of woodpeckers' holes, both to roost in and nest in. The whippoorwills are, like some nightjars (to which they are related) and some swifts and hummingbirds, remarkable in that for long periods during the winter they become torpid, although the thermometer may not fall below 64° F. In this state, when their body temperature is 55° F and their heartbeats are only detectable with a stethoscope, they sleep so deeply that they do not waken even when handled. The elf owls—no larger than fat sparrows—return by night from their southern winter quarters late in April or early in May, when the desert comes alive with, in Walker's words, "the wolf-whistles of the thrashers, the sad coos of mourning doves and the more sprightly notes of the white-wings; even the ground squirrels trill as tunefully as canaries"; and for a week or so after their arrival "their low whistles, puppy-like barks . . . issue from all regions where there are saguaros. Woodpeckers nesting in holes in these plants are continually disturbed at night by owls poking their heads in while searching for suitable nests."

8: Birds and Burrowers
of the Pampas

Venezuela and eastern Colombia have their tropical llanos, and the Brazilian highlands their campos of savannas and wooded slopes, but the South American counterpart of the steppes and prairies are the plains of Argentina—the pampas, whose quarter of a million square miles slope gradually from the Andes to the Atlantic. Broken only by low hills, the pampas merge in the north with the swampy savannas of the Gran Chaco and in the south with drought-resistant thorn scrub and desert. The fine-grained pampas soil, underlaid by rocklike "tosca" devoid of the smallest stones or pebbles, is hard and compacted, with the result that rain seldom penetrates beyond the top layer. Prior to the invasion of the pampas by European ranchers' tens of millions of sheep, cattle, and horses, the vegetation was dominated by the large and perennially deep-green tussocks, 3 or 4 feet high, of the tufted pampas grass whose myriads of flowering spears towered to a height of 8 or 9 feet, covering extensive areas with seas of fleecy white plumes, through which a horseman might ride for miles with the feathery spikes as high and higher than his head.

Although there were patches of scrub and woodland in damper hollows and woods of tala toward the wetter east coast, the pampas were and still are predominantly treeless, despite the introduction of the locust-immune eucalypti, with their bleached and peeling trunks, whose success disproved the theory that the violent pampero, which blows over the pampas at all seasons from the southwest, prevented trees from growing to any great height in the exceedingly rich soil, for the only large trees were the squat ombùs—with their soft spongy wood and poisonous laurel-like leaves—which never grew tall, though their massive trunks might girth 40 or 50 feet and shade the gleaming white estancia houses.

Treeless, windswept, subject to drought and extremes of temperature, the pampas afforded little covert from predators; therefore the herbivores, large and small, had to depend for survival on their fleetness of foot or their ability to live in burrows. But there was no parallel on the pampas to the immense aggregations of buffalo and antelope on the prairies or of the saiga and equines on the steppes, and only one large predator, the puma. There was indeed only one species of pampa deer and these grazed in pairs or small herds, especially on the extensive areas colonized by the cardoon or Castile thistle—the yellow-spined wild artichoke that grew in thick gray-green bushes 4 or 5 feet high. Yet in the nineteenth century the pampas provided pasture for eighty million sheep, cattle, and horses! Today, the total occupation of the pampas by ranchers and arable farmers has completely altered their ecological structure, and the deer are rare.

Where scrub invaded the more sparsely grassed pampas, a

vacant herbivorous niche was filled by the antelope-like maras—alias cavies or Patagonian hares—for they also inhabited the more barren Patagonian plateau, especially the extensive areas of brilliant yellow and rust-red gravel. They are becoming rarer both in Patagonia and on the pampas, partly because they are hunted for the pot and partly as a result of the introduction in 1887 of European brown hares which, with their astounding ability to thrive in so many different environments, now exist in plague numbers over the maras' entire range. Indeed, when motoring the length of Patagonia in 1971, Jeffrey Boswall estimated that he sighted a hare every 100 yards. Yet the maras are almost twice as large as hares, with relatively much longer legs, and have been compared with the blackbuck of India or the gazelles and impala of Africa, for their powerful hindquarters, with black and white blazon, and muscular hind legs (that enable them to accelerate to a top speed of about 40 miles per hour) terminate in three-toed feet whose heavy pads and claws somewhat resemble hooves; and Francisco Erize has described in an article in *Animals* how when threatened by a predator—usually a pampa fox—a mara bolts for its bush cover in a series of "rubber-legged" bounces and gigantic leaps, springing off its toes in the manner of an antelope and appearing to float through the air. Though living in large burrows, pairs and flocks of a dozen maras are aboveground most of the day and often at night, and according to Erize, spend much of their time basking catlike on their elbows in the sun or stretched out beside bushes.

Burrowing rodents were the predominant mammalian life on the pampas. Cuis or guinea pigs fed at dawn and dusk in groups of several hundred, and constructed nests at the bases of the grass tussocks. The rat-sized tuco-tuco, though requiring loose sandy soil in which it could "swim" like a mole beneath the surface, and therefore not ideally suited to the heavy moist mold of the pampas, was nevertheless present wherever there was a stretch of sandy soil or a range of dunes, regulating the temperature in its burrow, a foot or more below the surface and several yards long, by making openings to catch the prevailing winds, plugging them with grass in cold weather— "All day long and all night it sounds its voice, resonant and loud, like a succession of blows from a hammer," wrote W. H. Hudson.

It is astounding that we have to rely for much of our knowledge of pampas life on the observations of this naturalist who not only was born (a few miles from Buenos Aires) as long ago as 1841, but who also left the Argentine for good twenty-seven years later. That he did so was a tragedy both for himself and for natural history as he recognized toward the end of his life when in 1920 he wrote: "When I think of that land so rich in bird life . . . where I might have done so much . . . the reflection is forced upon me . . . that I probably made choice of the wrong road of the two then open to me."

The most conspicuous rodents on the pampas were the somewhat beaver-like vizcachas, which were already being decimated by landowners and ranchers before the end of the nineteenth century. Though also inhabiting regions to the north, south, and west of the pampas, and relatives of the chinchillas of the High Andes, the vizcachas were the pampas' counterparts of the prairie dogs, for their communities lived in villages or vizcacheras of closely grouped burrows covering 100 or 200 square feet and often sited on a slope overlooking a *laguna;* but whereas on stony "tosca" ground a community might include no more than four or five individuals, in soft, easily worked soil it might number a dozen or thirty. The members of vizcacheras would visit others in the vicinity, and no doubt all were related, for from time to time, according to Hudson, a male would leave its community and excavate a new burrow 40 or 50 yards away, though several months might elapse before it was joined by others and a new vizcachera established; but despite the fact that the two or three young in a litter were sexually mature when only three months old, a vizcacha population increased very slowly.

Some vizcacheras were reported to have been occupied for centuries and, like the townships of the prairie dogs, were so numerous that, in Hudson's experience, one might ride for 500 miles over the pampas and never traverse half a mile without seeing one or more villages.

The pitlike entrances to the vizcachas' cylindrical burrows were so large, being from 4 to 6 feet across and deep enough for a man to stand in, that cattle avoided treading over them, whereas the burrows of smaller rodents were likely to be trodden in, choked with debris, or flooded. The capacious mouths of the vizcacheras gave access to large circular chambers from 3 to 6 feet underground, with galleries diverging from these in all directions and in some cases communicating with those from other burrows. A vizcacha's digging technique varied according to whether it was working in hard "tosca," crumbling sand or gravel, or soft soil; though typically, according to Hudson, it excavated a hole 12 or 15 inches wide at an angle of about 25 degrees with the surface. But after digging down a few feet, it was no longer satisfied with merely scattering away the loose earth it fetched up, but cleared it away so far in a straight line from the entrance, and scratched so much along this line that it soon formed a trench a foot or more in depth, and often 3 or 4 feet in length. This facilitated the conveying of the loose earth as far as possible from the entrance, but in due course the spoil accumulated at the end of this long passage too, and the vizcacha would then scrape two additional trenches, converging into the passage, in the form of a capital Y.

As the excavation developed, so these trenches were also continually deepened and lengthened, and the angular segment of earth between them progressively scratched away until it, together with the spoil from the burrow, had been dumped in one huge, unsymmetrical mound, which might eventually be 30 or 40 feet in diameter and from 15 inches to several feet high.

Vizcacha—rodent of the pampas

The fact that these mounds, like those of the prairie dogs, protected vizcacheras sited on low-level ground from flooding was no doubt incidental to the primary necessity of getting rid of the spoil, since vizcacheras on high ground, where there was no risk of flooding, were also mounded. Hudson has described how in districts where, as far as the eye could see, the plains were level and smooth as a bowling-green, especially in winter when the grass was close-cropped, and where the rough giant thistle had not sprung up, the mounds appeared like brown or dark spots on a green surface. In some places they were so close together that from horseback he might count fifty or sixty, or even a hundred from one viewpoint.

One of the vizcachas' dominant impulses was to clear about half an acre of the rough growth of herbs and giant grasses surrounding their mounds, pulling these up by the roots and in so doing maintaining a smooth, close-shaven green turf which they grazed. The fact that this operation also served as a defense measure against predators, by providing the vizcachas with an extensive field of view, was again no doubt incidental, for they were possessed by a compulsion to cut down any tall plant they encountered. Acres of maize, for example, might be leveled, though left lying uneaten, and so too were posts if not hard enough to resist their chisel-like incisors.

The only exceptions to this compulsion were thistles when they were green, even though these might in the summer be growing in the vicinity of the burrows or, like the giant thistle, luxuriantly actually on the mounds. In this case the vizcachas were presumably repelled by the thistles' spikes or perhaps by their astringent sap. When the pampas burgeoned after the heavy October rains with a profusion of such flowers as verbena and oxalis, extensive areas of giant thistles, with variegated green and white leaves as large as those of rhubarb, surrounded estancias and within a couple of months formed dense thickets 6 to 10 feet high; while in "thistle years" they sprang up everywhere, covering most of the pampas. But when, as Hudson observed, the thistles withered and died, their huge hollow stalks as dry and light as the shaft of a bird's feather, though twice the circumference of a broomstick, transformed the pampas into a potential fire hazard.

If the thistles were not consumed by fire, however, then in March when the spikes were brittle, the vizcachas would level them by gnawing at their roots, and subsequently cut them up, tearing the huge flower heads to pieces and feasting on the seeds. Large patches of thistles might be dealt with in this way, until the ground was whitened with their silvery bristles, and every leveled stalk was dragged to and heaped around their mounds—as, for that matter, was every other transportable object, including mislaid whips, pistols, and knives. All were covered with excavated spoil and added to the height of the mounds, which in many cases were strewn with the skulls and bones of dead vizcachas that had been dragged out of their burrows. In contrast to the vizcachas, which selected the barest open levels for their villages, multitudes of opossums, weasels, skunks, and armadillos sheltered in the thickets of the perennial thistles, though when large hedges were planted on the pampas, these animals forsook the thistles and excavated their burrows under the hedges.

So long as green vegetation was available, the vizcachas did not require water, but after a long summer drought, during which they had subsisted for months on withered grass and bits of dried thistle stalks, they would venture out of their burrows as early as midday to drink eagerly from rainwater pools after a shower, though they did not normally emerge until shortly before sunset in the summer and seldom until dark in the winter. An adult male would usually appear first and sit for some time in a prominent position on his mound before beginning to feed; later other members of the community would station themselves at burrow entrances, with the very much smaller females (weighing only from 4 to 11 pounds in comparison with the 22-

pound males) sitting upright on their haunches, propped up by their tails. The underside of the basal part of the tail is padded with thick, bare, corneous kin, and with this a vizcacha would strike rapid warning blows on the ground; while, when startled at night by a loud noise such as a thunderclap or the report of a gun, a community would raise a tremendous outcry, ranging from the deepest booming to high shrieks and squeals.

The vizcachas' burrows, like those of prairie dogs, were ecologically vital to a number of pampas mammals, birds, reptiles, such as boas, and insects. The pampa fox, two species of wildcats, and the huron—a large weasel with offensive stink glands—were all almost entirely dependent on their burrows for earths, while maras and some armadillos often occupied abandoned burrows, though the only species of armadillo to thrive on the pampas because it was omnivorous, feeding on grass, birds' eggs and nestlings, insects, snakes, worms, and carrion, was the hairy armadillo. Scenting a grub several inches below the surface, this armadillo, instead of digging it up, would drive down its sharp snout and wedge-shaped head to the required depth, pitting the ground in this way with hundreds of conical bore holes. It also employed a unique method of killing snakes, squatting on them and, by swaying backward and forward, lacerating them with the sharp, serrated edges of its bony armor-plating.

Although the vizcachas were evicted from their burrows by foxes, they apparently accepted them, like the burrowing owls, as harmless members of the community; but the foxes, though preying mainly on cuis and rabbits, in fact killed the young vizcachas when these came aboveground in the spring, and might indeed decimate a village's entire population of young. The burrowing owls, though usually excavating their own nesting holes, made use of the vizcachas' mounds as lookout stations, as they did the prairie dogs', though also hovering 40 feet above the ground when hunting for mice, beetles, amphibians, and snakes up to 18 inches long; and all day long a pair of owls would pose close together bolt upright on a mound, motionless as statues except when their heads slowly rotated to watch a small rodent. Although the vizcachas paid no attention to the owls' hissing and beak-snapping when they approached too closely to them, they reacted to their alarm call at the appearance of a predator.

According to Hudson a number of insects that were very rare in other parts of the pampas were also associated with the vizcachas—notably bugs, six species of wingless wasps, and other wasps that preyed on spiders. The latter, which were very abundant on the pampas, included some extremely aggressive species. The monstrous, hairy, dark-brown *Myale fusca* would,

Wolf spider

for example, when approached, rear up erect on its four hinder feet and prepare to bite with its long, sickle-shaped black falces; while a still larger wolf spider would actually chase after a man on horseback passing within 3 or 4 feet of its lair.

In summer the pampas were the winterquarters of many immigrant birds whose breeding grounds lay far to the north or south—golden plover from the tundras of Canada and Alaska, together with godwit, redshank, and sandpipers, whose place was filled to a lesser degree during the pampas winter by plover and seed snipe from Patagonia; but resident terrestrial birds were few both in species and numbers, because of the lack of nesting and roosting cover and also of food, for there were few insects in the drier areas, while the large perennial grasses covering most of the pampas provided only limited quantities of seeds. Thus the mass of the pampas bird population comprised such waterfowl as ibises, flamingos, and storks concentrated around the lagunas, those shallow lakes of 300 or 400 acres largely choked with bright green sedges and vast beds of bullrushes. And two of the commonest pampas birds would have been extremely rare had it not been for the niches provided by the vizcachas' burrows, since in other habitats they nested in natural banks. Few vizcacheras were, for example, without their attendant miners, which excavated their nest holes in the bank-like sides of the burrows, while bank martins (or small swallows) took over the miners' previous year's nest holes. The bank martins fluttered about the burrowing owls with long complaining notes, and the miners ran about the bare ground around the vizcachas' burrows, occasionally uttering their shrill, laughter-like trills.

The introduction of ranching to the pampas also affected the birdlife. Cattle took the place of grazing deer in flushing insects for the cowbirds, and fence wires served them for display perches; burrowing owls used fencing posts as hunting lookouts, and flickers chipped nesting holes—some of which were usurped by white-rumped swallows—in posts and telegraph poles, just as the tree (brown-chested) martins appropriated the nests of the ovenbirds, usually those from which the young birds had flown, though if the owners' nesting was retarded, they were usually dispossessed. The ovenbirds were also victimized by the parasitical cowbirds, which preferred their nests to those of any other species as receptacles for their eggs. The red ovenbird was one of the commonest and most familiar birds of the pampas, for it nested by choice in the trees around estancias, and its large domed, globe-shaped, or oval nest structure of dried mud, resembling an old-fashioned baker's oven, was exposed for all to see on branches, house cornices, rocks, or fence posts. Measuring some 12 inches by 8, and weighing 8 or 9 pounds, its inch-thick walls were constructed of straw and vegetable fibers which, mixed with mud, formed a "reinforced concrete" capable of weathering two or three seasons' rains and droughts.

The introduction of the tall gum trees also encouraged the green, gray, and yellow monk parrakeets to colonize the pampas, though they were not welcome, for their flocks, several thousand strong, could devastate a plantation of maize as ruinously as the Carolina parrakeets did before they were exterminated. The colonies of monks constructed clusters of communal nests, in which each pair had its own compartment, suspended side by side from the ends of branches. Since one structure might be 9 feet long, the clusters formed dense tangles 6 feet or more in diameter and a quarter of a ton in weight, while a single gum might contain as many as eight such clusters.

Initially, ranching also benefited the most remarkable bird of the pampas, the crested screamer, a kind of gigantic lapwing as large as a turkey and armed on each wing with two formidable

pink spurs reputed to be capable of disemboweling a man—
though since there is no evidence that the birds fought with
these, it is difficult to understand what purpose they served.
The chajas or chakars, as they were colloquially known, were
essentially birds of marsh and well-watered pampas, wading,
swimming, and walking with the aid of their long toes over the
floating mats of water hyacinth, while feeding on the leaves and
seeds of aquatic plants; but according to Hudson, when the indigenous coarse grasses were replaced by soft clovers and grasses
from the Old World, the chakars throve on these, until the new
immigrants, especially the Italians, "the pitiless enemies of all
birdlife," slaughtered them for the pot. And Hudson was probably the last naturalist to witness a whole plain covered with endless flocks of chakars, scattered in pairs and small groups. Although it was the height of the dry season at the time, much
standing water still remained in rushy pools, and this factor no
doubt accounted for this concentration.

At any hour of the day and at any season of the year, though
especially on calm sunny days in winter and spring, the chakars
had the remarkable habit, considering their great size and the
difficulty they had in taking off into flight, of soaring in immense spirals on their 6½-foot spread of wings, while singing at
intervals, until disappearing from sight in a clear sky:

> The male begins [wrote Hudson in *The Naturalist in La Plata*],
> the female takes up her part, and then with marvellous
> strength and spirit they pour forth a torrent of strangely-
> contrasted sounds—some bassoonlike in their depth and vol-
> ume, some like drum-beats, and others long, clear and ring-
> ing. It is the loudest animal-sound of the pampas. . . . Their
> resounding choral notes reach the distant earth clarified with a
> rhythmic swell and fall as of chiming bells. They also sing by
> night at three-hourly intervals—"counting the hours", the

gauchos say; and where they have congregated together in tens of thousands the mighty roar of their combined voices produces an astonishingly grand effect.

The chakars also sang from the ground, and Hudson goes on to describe how, when traveling alone one summer day, he came at noon to a lake on the pampas—a sheet of water narrow enough for him to see across:

Chakars in countless numbers were gathered along its shores, but they were all ranged in well-defined flocks, averaging about five hundred birds in each flock. These flocks seemed to extend all round the lake, and had probably been driven by the drought from all the plains around to this spot. Presently one flock near me began singing, and continued their powerful chant for three or four minutes; when they ceased the next flock took up the strains, and after it the next, and so on until the notes of the flocks on the opposite shore came floating strong and clear across the water—then passed away, growing fainter and fainter, until once more the sound approached me travelling round to my side again. . . . I was astonished at the orderly way with which each flock waited its turn to sing, instead of a general outburst taking place after the first flock had given the signal.

He also writes of his surprise at the behavior of a pair of chakars during a thunderstorm:

On a still sultry day in summer I was standing watching masses of black cloud coming rapidly over the sky, while a hundred yards from me stood the two birds also apparently watching the approaching storm with interest. Presently the edge of the cloud touched the sun, and a twilight gloom fell on the earth. The very moment the sun disappeared the birds rose up and soon began singing their long-resounding notes, though it was loudly thundering at the time, while vivid flashes of lightning lit the black cloud overhead at short intervals. I watched their flight and listened to their notes, till suddenly as they made a wide sweep upwards they disappeared in the cloud, and at the same moment their voices became muffled. . . . The cloud continued emitting sharp flashes of lightning, but the birds never reappeared, and after six or seven minutes once more their notes sounded loud and clear above the muttering thunder.

One of the ecological niches on the open pampas, from southern Brazil to Patagonia, left vacant by the absence of large herds of ungulates, was also filled by a bird—the rhea, which associated in flocks of from half a dozen to exceptionally fifty while feeding almost exclusively on grasses and grain, though also on insects, especially grasshoppers. Now greatly reduced in numbers by the spread of agriculture, rheas, it has been said, were better adapted to pampas conditions than any other birds because, standing 5 feet or more above the ground, they could see predators at a great distance and, being wary and difficult to approach, run more swiftly from them than a galloping horse, while their pale grayish-blue plumage camouflaged them in the pampas haze. Inexplicably, the pampas rheas, or ñandús, ran with one wing raised like a sail, whereas the smaller, pearly-gray Darwin's rheas, inhabiting the eastern slopes of the Andes, often in company with guanacos, lifted both wings vertically, one after the other, when accelerating into a zigzag course with neck stretched out almost horizontally and feet coming up high with every step. But what were these predators? We know that pumas, which were certainly very numerous in Patagonia, if not on the pampas (from which they have now been banished to the Andes), killed sitting rheas and ate their eggs, as did foxes and wildcats; but the solitary-living, red-maned wolves, of whose habits we are still almost wholly ignorant, lived mainly in partly wooded country to the north of the pampas, and in any case preyed predominantly on small mammals.

Hudson has described how at the approach of the breeding season the mature, black-necked cock rheas became extremely aggressive, attacking the immature cocks in the flock and driving them away, and also fighting with other adult cocks: "The combattants twisting their long necks together like a couple of serpents, and then viciously biting at each other's heads with their beaks; meanwhile they turn round and round in a circle, pounding the earth with their feet, so that where the soil is wet or soft they make a circular trench where they tread."

Having established by conquest his harem of half a dozen hens, the cock, standing with raised and agitated wings among the tall plumed grasses, would call them together with hollow booms and long-drawn-out suspirations, ventriloquial in character, as if, in Hudson's words, "a wind blowing high up in the void sky had found a voice"; for it was the cock who incubated for six weeks the 12 or 30 or as many as 120 eggs laid by his various hens in the unlined and exposed natural hollow that served for a nest, though if he became broody before all the hens had finished laying, he drove them away to, perforce, drop their eggs randomly in large numbers. It was the cock, too, who, if the nest was threatened, lured the predator away, trailing outspread wings. He also cared for and defended the chicks for six weeks after they hatched, charging with neck outstretched and wings spread at a man on horseback, and warding off the attacks of crowned and harpy eagles and the carrion hawks—the caranchas (or caracaras), which also gathered in seventies or eighties to gorge on the carcasses of deer, and occasionally, no doubt, the chimangos, though these were mainly scavengers, preying only on sickly animals and on reptiles, amphibians, and insects, including locusts. Since they were comparatively weak fliers, they captured these by running or jumping after them and killing them with blows of their hooked beaks. Chimangos are still the commonest birds of prey over extensive areas of the pampas, often soaring and performing aerial evolutions, thirty or forty together, and flocking in hundreds and possibly thousands to cultivated land, where they follow the plow like rooks.

9: Survival in the Australian Desert and Grasslands

More than one-third of Australia's landmass is desert. In the vast interior is the Red Centre, where sand, soil, and most rocks are colored a fiery cinnabar. Surrounding the Centre are plains of clay and sandy loam, and within both desert and plain regions are the gibber flats, strewn with stones stained with iron oxide and scoured and polished by wind-driven grains of sand. But the Australian desert, the second largest on earth, is semi-arid rather than proper desert. True, the vegetation is sparse and stunted, and large areas are totally lacking in surface water, but tracts of hundreds and, in some regions, thousands of square miles to the north of the Centre are blue-green or gray with the foliage of mulgas, those dwarf acacias reaching 30 feet in height and blossoming after any heavy shower of rain with a riotous bloom of deliciously scented, golden-yellow bottle brushes. And everywhere delicate plants lie dormant in the sand and among the sand-sculptured rocks awaiting the very rare fall of "winter" rain: ephemeral plants, like those of the steppes, able to germinate, flower, and seed within a very short period—drought-escaping rather than drought-resistant. Within ten to fourteen days of rain falling, the sands are carpeted with greenery or with vivid scarlet sweeps of the Sturt pea.

Here and there the gray "forests" of mulgas are splashed with the clear green foliage of ironwood trees, and alternate with equally extensive areas of the spiny spinifex or porcupine grass growing in clumps of giant pincushions from 1 to 6 feet high and 6 to 20 feet across, gray-green after rain, pale golden during drought. One of several species of the xerophytic *Triodia* (of which another species, the true spinifex, grows only on the white sand), the porcupine grass is crowned with tall heads of spun-gold seeds on which small finches and doves feed, and which also provide nourishing fodder for cattle, who during periods of prolonged drought may browse the plant so heavily that it does not recover for a long time. The most inflammable vegetation in the Australian bush, even the tips of the "darning-needle" spines that bristle from the plant's outer surface, are impregnated like wax matches, while the network of oily stems explode, billowing smoke when a match is thrown into the bush.

The distribution of the various types of vegetation is determined by the amount and seasonal regularity of the rainfall and to the south of the central deserts, though still on the red sand and extending in a broad belt from east to west, is the Mallee country, where sapling-sized eucalypti with multiple trunks cling to hillsides and mingle with the mulgas and spinifex that dominate the arid and semiarid regions. Where there is red sand the mallee gums infiltrate the great plains of silver and blue-gray saltbush which, under favorable conditions, grows knee-high or shoulder-high. Mulgas, 100-foot desert oaks or casuarinas with dark drooping plumes and trunks that appear jet black against the bare red sand, corkwoods, and ironwoods in groups of five or ten or in parklands are scattered over the sandhills and plains; red river gums line the watercourses, and chalk-white ghost gums with brilliant green foliage grow singly on red and yellow or purple-green rocky outcrops.

Lizards dart through clumps of spinifex, freshened by a shower of rain; geckos prey on the termites that inhabit the spinifex and build mounds 20 feet or more in height, with flying buttresses projecting from the central structure and subterranean tunnels extending for hundreds of yards as feeding ways. At night thousands of tiny green reflections along the beam of a flashlight are the eyes of the phenomenal numbers of wolf spiders that inhabit the desert, retreating during the day into vertical shafts sealed with lids matching the surrounding sand.

Central Australia, with its almost total lack of surface water, would, like the deserts of the American Southwest, appear to be totally unsuited to an amphibian's requirements. Even its "lakes," 100 square miles or more in extent, are dry and covered with a fine layer of gypsum. Yet, after heavy falls of rain, numerous frogs enliven the nights with their croaking from the temporary pools, and there are in fact half a dozen species of desert frogs which have overcome their peculiar environmental problems by aestivating deep underground or at the base of hollow trees during the long droughts, restricting their active life to the few weeks in the year when there is surface water. The most ingenious of these frogs is *Chivonectes platycephalus*, and Allen Keast has described in *Australia and the Pacific Islands* how, prior to aestivating, this, the water-holding frog, stores water in its urinary bladder and body cavity, distending itself to the size of a tennis ball:

A foot to eighteen inches below the drying mud at the bottom of the pond it secretes a capsule of mucus about itself and this provides additional protection against desiccation. In this way it can apparently withstand droughts of a year or more. As soon as the land is flooded again it comes to the surface. Breeding follows immediately, the tadpole stage possibly being as short as two weeks. Metamorphosis has to be completed before the pond dries up; those individuals that have been lucky enough not to have fallen prey to the herons, which arrive with the rains, will become air-breathing frogs and be able to take shelter underground.

Lying in a wide arc around the central deserts to east and north are relatively limited stretches of temperate grasslands dotted with trees growing singly or in clusters, though cattle stations, some of which cover 8000 square miles, may be almost entirely grass. Although the large hill kangaroos—the handsome, red-brown euros or roan wallaroos with pure white throats and chests—living on the lower slopes of the ranges, browse quite extensively on the porcupine grass, there are no large herds of deer, antelope, buffalo, or equines (except for the Timor horses of the Northern Territory, the feral brumbies) to graze the Australian grasslands, and therefore very few plants except the spinifex are protected by spines. Small mobs of kangaroos and emus replace the large herbivores of North America, Africa, and Asia, just as the rock wallabies, inhabiting those gigantic isolated outcrops of rock that are such an extraordinary feature of the flat Australian plains, could be considered the counterparts of mountain sheep and goats; while the now very rare hare wallabies or maalas took the place of true hares (prior to the introduction about 1870 of the European brown hares), lying out by day in forms, or in rudimentary burrows a foot or two deep, beneath the arching pincushions of porcupine grass, feeding on the spines and living exclusively in areas of pure spinifex.

The fact that browsing animals and thorny plants are in the minority in Australia could be considered as confirming the theory that plants have evolved thorns and spines as a protection against browsing, but on the other hand thorniness is most developed in arid deserts where herbivores are least common. Conversely, the fruits of plants such as the prickly pear, though armored with small, thickly set tufts of minute but very sharp barbed hairs, easily detachable, are eaten in large quantities by mice and ground squirrels. It seems more likely that in fact thorniness is the physical result of a dry atmosphere and drought conditions.

There are some fifty different species of kangaroo-like marsupials, ranging from the 12-inch-long rat kangaroos to the giant reds, 4½ feet tall when "squatting" and 6 feet when erect. The larger species are exclusively herbivorous, with grass forming the bulk of their food, and where the grazing is good are numerous in sheltered valleys in the mountains; but they also thrive on coarse, unnutritious forage on which few other large herbivores could subsist, and are therefore very widely distributed over the drier areas of the Centre, including the stony ridges of relatively unimproved cattle stations, where the grass grows only after the sporadic rains. They also inhabit the semi-desert with less than 20 inches of rain of the saltbush country, and the sandy mallee and mulga plains, where pairs or very small mobs of a smaller and paler-colored race of the big reds usually forage in the scrub, except when a flush of grass springs up after localized storms, resting in the shade of the trees during the heat of the day, grazing at dusk, and possibly drinking only every third day.

The large wallaroos, which live in drought regions with very little vegetation, can survive without water for fourteen days or longer because, like true desert dwellers, they are able to con-

Wallaroo doe with joey in pouch

serve body fluids by forming concentrated urine and, lacking
sweat glands, endeavor to cool off, if temperatures rise to critical levels, by panting and licking their forearms. By contrast,
the gray kangaroos, though living in the scrublands bordering

the big reds' habitat and grazing in the open woodlands that are better watered, drink three times as often as the reds which, feeding out on the grasslands in the early morning, the evening, and at night in mobs of usually less than ten, sometimes congregate in thirties or even fifties to drink at cattle station tanks. During the hot noonday the reds retreat into the shade of the light casuarina scrub, where they stretch out at full length on sides or backs, twitching long-eared heads against the tormenting flies, half closing their eyes, and throwing occasional pawfuls of dust over heads and shoulders.

In the 1940s an ecologist, Francis Ratcliffe, encountered family groups of reds everywhere in the South Australia sheep country. These usually comprised one very large, wine-red buck or boomer, with one or two smoky, blue-gray does or "blue fliers" considerably smaller than the bucks, two or more juveniles, and a single young joey. When disturbed they would string out, zigzagging through the bluebushes at 30 miles per hour, with the bucks leaping 12 feet with every jerking bound, the does barely seeming to touch the ground, and the joey "bouncing manfully along beside or behind or spurting ahead with an absurd, frantic rocking-horse action." When moving slowly a kangaroo swings its hind legs forward between the arch formed by forelegs and tail; when it hops, its body is inclined forward and balanced on hind legs and tail, which does not touch the ground; and when "boxing" another male, a kangaroo can in fact balance solely on its tail while striking with its hind legs.

No doubt a kangaroo's leaping powers have been exaggerated. Graham Pizzey, for example, questions whether they can in fact bound more than 15 feet or leap fences more than 4 feet high, and states that they tire after traveling more than a mile or two at 20 miles per hour. Certainly many are found dead in wire fences. But a large boomer's 4- to 6-foot stride rapidly lengthens with increasing speed into a 26-foot stride, and there is evidence that it can in fact leap 42 feet and clear a 10-foot fence when hunted; while other observers state that it can maintain a speed of 25 miles per hour over long distances and accelerate to 30 or 40 miles per hour. Recent experiments have shown that at speeds greater than 10 miles per hour a kangaroo's peculiar gait uses up less energy than the conventional gait of a quadruped of the same weight, and this factor may possibly have contributed to its survival when other marsupials of conventional gait became extinct after the arrival of the aborigines and their dingoes.

In the 1950s the population of reds was at a peak, but in the years 1954–65 more than seven million red, gray, and hill kangaroos were slaughtered in Queensland alone, despite the now well-proven fact that kangaroos compete only minimally with sheep, since even during severe droughts the latter subsist mainly on herbs and not grasses. The disastrous drought of 1964–66 probably resulted in a further drastic reduction in their numbers, and when in June and July 1965 Pizzey traveled 6000 miles from Melbourne to the Gulf of Carpentaria and thence across to the Queensland coast, he saw less than a dozen live reds. Although dingoes and wedge-tailed eagles kill a few adults of the smaller kangaroos and wallabies and may take a heavy toll of the joeys, their numbers have never been controlled by predators. According to Le Soeuf, sand flies were responsible for a certain mortality, for these flies, which swarm in certain regions after rain, sting the kangaroo's eyelids when they are drinking at water holes, causing these to swell up and ultimately inducing blindness and the death by starvation of small mobs.

The major natural controller of the kangaroo population has always been drought, and in drought years more than three-

quarters of the joeys may die because the does lack milk. However the does are able to counter this sporadic natural hazard
(though not that of man's ruthless persecution) by producing
young at any season of the year, and by being extraordinarily
prolific. One large-scale research operation in New South
Wales, for example, involving the examination of twenty-five
hundred does, revealed that 75 percent of them had young in
the pouch. Reaching their full size in about four years, whereas
the bucks require ten years, the does are capable of breeding
when only two years old and of having, at one and the same
time, one joey at foot and another in the pouch, while also being
pregnant with a third. They can therefore produce four joeys
every three years.

Several kinds of rodents live in the grasslands, among them
the stick-nest rats, resembling small rabbits with rats' tails,
whose communal nests of sticks are firmly interlocked into a
compact, beehive-shaped cone. Nests are 4 feet in diameter and
3 feet high, and contain enough material to fill three or four
large wheelbarrows. The only Australian rats to reach plague
numbers sporadically over areas of 50,000 square miles are,
however, the long-haired rats, and these do so only at intervals
of thirty or perhaps sixty years, when wedge-tailed eagles and
black kites feed almost exclusively on them. There are also
various marsupial mice, including the nocturnal hopping mice,
whose long legs enable them, like jerboa pouched mice and jerboa rats, to leap swiftly, though they normally progress on all
fours. Jerboa mice can bound 5 or 6 feet, but what advantage do
they and the jerboa rats gain by being able to leap like
kangaroos? Both are too small to be able to clear the large grass
tussocks and shrubs of their arid sandy habitat, where the great
sandhill ridges are crisscrossed with their footprints, and in
which they must survive for months at a time without water.

Possibly this mode of progression is confusing to predatory birds, though the true nonhopping mice survive equally successfully in the same habitat. By contrast, the rabbit-sized rat kangaroo of the plains "floats" along at the speed of a galloping horse on its long, spindly hind legs, with tiny forelegs folded into its chest, balancing with tail half as long again as its body, though not much thicker than a pencil. H. H. Finlayson recounts how he was obliged to use three fresh horses before finally running one down after a 12-mile chase.

Until "rediscovered" east of Lake Eyre by Finlayson in 1930, the plains rat kangaroo had been supposed extinct for eighty-five years, yet it is not an inconspicuous animal, since it does not burrow but survives the searing heat of the Australian desert in a flimsy shelter of grass and leaves in a shallow hollow on the open stony or sandy plain or under a bush. The nest is thatched with twigs and grass stems, through which the rat thrusts its head from time to time to observe the outside world—a habit of which the aboriginals take advantage by noting the location of the opening and creeping up on the opposite side. A graphic description of the summer heat in the plains rat kangaroo's habitat was recorded in *Narrative of an Expedition into Central Australia* by Charles Sturt who, when exploring the desert east of Lake Eyre 130 years ago, experienced mean shade temperatures of 101 to 104° F day after day throughout the months of December, January, and February:

> Under its effects every screw in our boxes had been drawn, and the horn handles of our instruments, as well as our combs, were split into fine laminae. The lead dropped out of our pencils . . . our hair, as well as the wool on the sheep [his meat on the hoof], ceased to grow, and our nails had become as brittle as glass.

Also inhabiting both the grasslands and the deserts of the Red

Centre are the rabbit bandicoots or bilbies, though it is possible that all have now been driven from the grasslands by the alien rabbits (introduced in the mid-nineteenth century) which, finding it difficult to scratch out burrows in the rubbly soil, evicted the bilbies from their warrens, associated with a vigorous growth of bush. Any countryman over the age of twenty has seen at firsthand the damage to pasture, crops, and woodlands of which rabbits are capable in their natural habitat, extending from Scandinavia to North Africa; but this damage is relatively minor in comparison with the devastation they have wrought in countries such as Australia to which they have been introduced, for rabbits, despite their vulnerability to disease and innumerable predators, have been one of the most successful of mammals, penetrating even the Red Centre. In the deserts they served to provide food, and also pupping dens, for large numbers of dingoes, which Sturt reported to be in a very emaciated condition and not very numerous in the Interior in the prerabbit era of the 1840s.

Ratcliffe, in reporting in *Flying Fox and Drifting Sand* on the horrific nature of the rabbits' sporadic population explosions in Australia, described one occasion when a horde of rabbits, irrupting from the sandhill country in the north, descended upon a cattle range in such millions that the ground seemed to move with them. Pits were dug along the wire-netting check fence, but these were rapidly filled with the crushed and smothered corpses of the firstcomers, piled up to the top of the netting, as the horde clambered over them and over the fence, to tumble down on the other side and swarm on southward.

The fact that the equally successfully introduced red foxes—themselves decimated by mange when multiplying excessively—were never able to exterminate local populations of rabbits reduced to remnant stocks by drought illustrates once again that prey populations are never ultimately controlled by predators; nor did myxomatosis, initially introduced into Australia in 1950, decimate the rabbits until widespread flooding produced the requisite numbers of mosquitoes as vectors of the virus.

10: Australian Desert and Plains Birds

The only grassland fauna comparable in stature to the larger kangaroos are the emus, which are larger than rheas, though they are variable in size, with the 100-pound hens—slightly taller than the cocks—standing 6 feet when rearing up aggressively. Like the cock rheas, the cock emus call up their harems of hens with a resonant drumming, and are responsible for the greater part of the seven weeks' incubation of the eggs, and subsequently for the protection of the dozen or score of young birds for a further eighteen months. Although emus, like kangaroos, have been mercilessly persecuted—more than 280,000 were slaughtered in Western Australia alone between 1945 and 1960—they are still comparatively numerous away from closely settled areas, and are usually encountered in ones and twos pacing alongside fences, with their bearlike plumage flopping with every colossal stride, while feeding on grass,

grain, fruits such as quandong, and immense numbers of caterpillars and insects.

When traveling fast, however, with neck stretched forward
and feet appearing to pause for a fraction of a second before each
powerful backward drive, an emu can run at 25 miles an hour
for some miles and is capable of much higher speeds, for Ratcliffe states that on one occasion he had to accelerate to over 40
miles per hour before forcing one to swerve to one side of his
car. The unanswerable question is why, in the absence of large
predators in Australia, have emus developed such speed? At the
present time they are preyed on to a limited extent by dingoes
and wedge-tailed eagles, but all the evidence points to dingoes
being comparative newcomers to Australia, probably immigrat-
ing with the aboriginals perhaps twenty thousand years ago, and
being feral rather than indigenous wild dogs, for they are not
markedly different from yellowish or black sheep or cattle dogs,
except for their permanently erect ears and brushy tails, and the
fact that though they yelp and howl and yodel when hunting,
they do not bark. As Frederick Jones Wood wrote some fifty
years ago:

> The Dingo, even in the most remote places, has still a curious
> hankering after man and his fleshpots. He still falls in behind
> the buggy, still follows the traveller at a discreet distance, still
> has a leaning towards hanging on to his camp—and this de-
> spite the fact that he is always killed at sight for the price set
> on his scalp.

The daily and seasonal lives of the birds that inhabit the
deserts and dry plains, with their sporadic or years-long
droughts, are controlled by their need for water, though, according to Stanley Breeden, a number of desert species such as
wrens, thornbills, redthroats, and crested bellbirds do not mi-

Emu

grate in search of water, surviving by conserving energy and by such adaptations as taking full advantage of shade, flying as little as possible, and hunting for food during the cooler hours of the day. Moreover, some desert birds are known to lose much less water when breathing than do their counterparts in more favorable climates.

However, wherever surface water occurs in the desert, birds congregate, mainly those such as finches, pigeons, doves, and parrots that cannot survive without a daily drink, but not crows, bustards, or emus; and enormous flocks of some species gather to drink at water holes and stock-dams and tanks. Vincent Serventy estimated that half a million budgerigars (shell parrots) were massed at one pool, and concentrations of sixty thousand cockatoos, including both pink-and-grey galahs and pure white corellas, have also been recorded. The large numbers of bores sunk along stock routes and on cattle stations in recent years must have benefited and also influenced the distribution of several species, particularly galahs, zebra finches, and crested pigeons and most notably the flock pigeons, which formerly swarmed in countless thousands over the grasslands of the tropical interior, but disappeared during the earlier decades of the present century. They were then believed to be extinct, but have now reappeared in flocks of hundreds and occasionally thousands.

Water for stock is stored in large surface tanks with earthen walls, and run off into shallow lateral troughs; and Michael Sharland has described in an article in *Animals* how the pigeons usually arrive at a tank from all parts of the sun-baked plain during the last hour of daylight, when the sun is dipping low and the shadow of the bore windmill reaches out across the cattle-pugged surface of the ground. According to him, stockmen and other observers believe that the pigeons' drinking hour is governed by the position of the sun, and their final dash to the water is triggered off by the sun touching the edge of the horizon. He suggests that, if they arrived after the sun had set, waiting predators would not be visible in the brief twilight that follows. Sunset is apparently the only time when the pigeons drink, and they do so only during the very short interval between the sun touching the horizon and setting. The first to arrive do so in small groups of ten or fifteen, but, writes Sharland:

> As the sun touched the edge of the distant plain and illuminated the earth banks of a station bore with orange-red . . . there was a demented rush to drink as great numbers whined above my head, all having come in together, two thousand or so of them. . . .
>
> They all sought to drink at once. The earth walls seemed to move with bodies closely packed, as wave after wave walked down to the edge to drink, those behind pushing others out of their way. There was scarcely a space for all at the water's edge, so a number rose, encircled the tank, and then, surprisingly, alighted on the surface of the water. Floating like seagulls, they drank their fill. I would never have believed that pigeons could do that—and still be able to rise again before becoming waterlogged.
>
> [Then] this great grey-brown . . . sheet of bodies rose, from banks and water . . . and swept into the sky. For at that moment the sun's light had been shut off. The shadows disappeared, and merged into twilight.

During prolonged periods of great heat, when temperatures may reach 116° F for sixteen consecutive days, thousands of birds may be drowned by the sheer pressure of numbers at a drinking pool, and there is a report of sixty thousand budgerigars being drowned in one small dam in such circumstances. Pizzey has described in an article in *Animals* how at a camp beside a small pool formed by the overflow of a bore-filled tank, he was awakened before dawn by a rushing blizzard of chirruping, and during the next hour wave after wave of budgerigars came streaming in to cluster over several dead mulga trees:

> Then as the sun came over the horizon, they started to wheel and dive over the water in a green vortex, dropping to drink, and then fluttering up at the last moment, until finally . . . they swarmed down as though poured from a pitcher, many alighting on the shallow water and gulping as they lay spread on the surface. This went on for several hours, and in that time 10,000 may have drunk. Finally the pool was reduced almost to a sheet of wet mud.

The dense flocks of budgerigars, cockatoos, and other species are awaited at their watering places by the predators—falcons, goshawks, black-shouldered kites, even dingoes. Their defense is to drink at dawn or dusk only, or to approach the water on foot from a distance; to whirl around the pool in massed thousands, rendering it difficult for a raptor to cut out a single individual; or, like grass finches and pigeons, to suck up water quickly instead of swallowing a beakful at a time. The budgerigars display no fear of man, but if, writes Stanley Breeden, "a falcon or a goshawk appears . . . the budgerigars erupt into a vivid green cloud and speed away in a tight, fast flock . . . dodging and weaving in the sunlight"; and Pizzey has described how during the peak of the rush to drink at his camping pool, a little falcon and a pair of black falcons waited overhead, and made slashing stoops down into the flocks of terrified budgerigars, which opened to let them pass, and rushed hard-flying and silent off and around the treetops:

> Finally the little falcon dashed at a leafy bush bulging with birds, beat over it for a moment until one budgerigar tried to

flee, and seized it in midair before it had gone ten yards. But such was the compulsion among the thirsty small seed-eaters that within minutes they were wheeling back over the water again.

In drier regions where larger prey may be scarce, even the magnificent wedge-tailed eagles may stoop into the flocks of budgerigars, smashing down numbers with their wings, spanning 7 feet, before pulling up and turning to pick up the dead and injured, if not forestalled by the falcons and kites and spotted harriers which, nesting in gums along dry watercourses, are the only harriers in the world to nest in trees. Normally, the wedgetails are mainly rabbit and carrion eaters, though also taking a heavy toll of dingo pups and preying on red foxes—the only predator to do so—and on the 6-foot-long, brown and yellow sand goannas that hunt over the sandhills in the cooler hours from one snake's or rat's or lizard's burrow to the next, investigating their entrances with their long forked tongues and digging down into them with a powerful rippling action of their claws if they are occupied.

Water holes are essential to the birds of the deserts and arid lands not only as drinking sources, but also for the actual survival of their species. Since most of them are obliged to travel considerable distances to the few scattered pools, their assemblies at these become social gatherings for such activities as mutual preening, courtship, and mating. Most desert birds are probably nomadic rather than migratory and, being continually on the move in their search for food, are always prompt to enter a district in which rain has fallen.

Breeden has described how chats, wood swallows, budgerigars, and quail will suddenly arrive in an area where there has been rain, breed intensively while the food supply lasts, and then disappear as suddenly as they came. Within hours of a shower of rain, budgerigars and wood swallows are courting, and within a week the seed-eating zebra finches—probably the most numerous birds in the Australian desert, though their flocks are seldom more than a dozen or perhaps fifty strong—are laying eggs; but though a fall of rain results in a temporary abundance of plant and insect food, such falls are both sporadic and infrequent, and nest building, incubation, and the rearing of the young must be completed before food becomes scarce again. Budgerigars, for example, which nest in holes in trees in colonies of up to a dozen pairs—almost every large mallee in some districts houses from one to five pairs—hatch their clutches of four to eight eggs in seventeen days, while the nestlings fledge in about six weeks and are reported to be in mating condition eight weeks later.

In the 1930s Finlayson could describe the flocks of budgerigars circling around the water holes in the Red Centre as assessable in acres rather than in thousands; but although there has been a catastrophic decrease in their numbers from their former tens of millions, they still range throughout the Interior in flocks of a dozen or several hundreds, "marching" across the arid plains while sifting the sand for grass seeds, twittering noisily in the trees at water holes. Only when assembling to drink at tanks during droughts or when collecting for migration do they now concentrate in thousands, for according to Allen Keast, "They move north in the autumn and return southward in the spring, the former bringing them to the country watered by the summer monsoon and the latter to where the winter rains assure good spring conditions. But . . . they do not return to the same place each time, being abundant in a district one year and completely absent from it the next."

"The desert," writes Breeden, "painted in reds, browns and yellows receives added colour . . . from the many species of

parrots and the huge flocks of corella and galah cockatoos."
There are still possibly tens of millions of cockatoos, feeding in
flocks of a thousand on grass seeds, bulbs, and roots, and performing swift-moving and exuberant aerobatics at dusk, while
wheeling in tight formation and screeching in deafening discord,
before settling to roost with full crops containing thirty thousand grass seeds.

11: Birds and Insects
of the African Savannas

A third of Africa's 11½ million square miles is savanna, merging in the north into the near-desert steppe of the Sudan, and extending southward through the high-altitude grasslands around the Great Lakes of East Africa to Zambia, Rhodesia, Mozambique, and the South African veld.

Savanna, a tropical or subtropical type of steppe, can only develop in those regions where an annual rainfall of from 20 to 50 inches, concentrated in one period of months, is followed by a prolonged dry season associated with grass fires, though the incidence of rain and drought is erratic. Were rainfall distributed evenly throughout the year, large tracts of savanna would be colonized by a dense tangle of bush, reducing the area of pasture available to herbivores, whereas the savannas are largely extensive plains of tall grasses, "brushed with delicate strokes of buff and rose and yellow-green yet predominantly lion-blond," as Evelyn Ames has described them in *A Glimpse of Eden*, and studded with termite mounds, thorny acacias "whose feathery leaves," in George Schaller's words, "diffuse the harshness of the sun," and such drought-resistant trees as cactus-like euphorbias and solitary baobabs. A thousand, two thousand years old perhaps, the swollen, glossy, purplish-gray boles, some more than 45 feet in circumference, of the baobabs rise in tapering columns for 15 or 20 feet and then split into a number of large branches, so that when leafless before the rains they present the appearance of roots pointing to the sky. Only along riverbanks is there dense bush or forest where, to quote from Evelyn Ames again, "the yellow-barked acacia makes a delicate chartreuse screen broken here and there by a sausage-tree, rough-barked and muscled as an old oak, hung the two-foot pods which give it its name."

All life on the African savannas is controlled by the irregular pattern of rainfall and drought. This balance or imbalance influences insect populations which affect much of the plant life and therefore animal environment. Army worms, for example, which include the caterpillars of a number of species of moths, sporadically swarm over the savannas in aggregations of thousands of millions, and are almost as devastatingly destructive as locusts were before they were largely brought under control—temporarily at any rate—in the 1940s. By contrast tsetse flies render cattle ranching permanently impracticable over large areas, and thus not only preserve these from overgrazing and soil erosion, but also conserve them as natural sanctuaries for the great herds of indigenous game.

Insects may have a direct effect on animal populations, as when in 1962, after floods had followed a drought and created swamps out of dried-up lake beds, a plague of biting flies on the plains of Tanzania's Ngorongoro Crater so incapacitated the lions that, though attempting to escape them by climbing into trees and crawling into hyena earths, the majority became emaciated, pockmarked with bloody bare spots. Some died, others emigrated to the nearby Serengeti plains where the flies were not numerous enough to be harmful, and the Ngorongoro population dropped from seventy to fifteen, though by 1969 it was up to seventy again, mainly as a result of an exceptionally high survival rate among the cubs.

Termites perform the tasks of earthworms in temperate regions, cultivating the soil and mixing it with plant debris. Those iridescent blue-green scarabs, the dung beetles, after emerging from their underground cocoons at the onset of the rains, also fertilize the soil by breaking up animal droppings and burying them. They "home" onto fresh dung almost as soon as it hits the ground, and Norman Carr has described in *Return to the Wild* how these beetles, having picked up the wind-borne smell of a buffalo kill, would fly in like overloaded bombers and crash-land heavily near the carcass: "Their radar or smelling organs must be efficient, for they were flying in continuously the whole time and were there in profusion."

Carr goes on to describe how, patting and molding portions of dung, from the stomach contents strewn around, into "golf balls" much larger than themselves, the dung beetles roll and trundle these away industriously by moving backward while rotating the balls with their hind legs and pushing so energetically and rapidly with heads bowed to the ground that they often overbalance; but they tenaciously continue pushing their cumbersome spoils over formidable obstacles, following a tortuous route for a hundred yards or so until they arrive at a suitably soft patch of ground. There, they excavate the soil around and beneath the dung ball until it is buried, and lay an egg in a hole in the top of it. The dung remains moist underground, and the

Dung beetles

larva, when it hatches, eats away the interior and ultimately pupates within the thin outer shell.

Even the tiniest, less than 0.79 inches long, of Africa's more than two thousand species of dung beetles, can bury 6.1 cubic inches of dung during the course of a night; they illustrate the profound effect the presence or absence of the smallest creature can have on an environment's ecology. There were, for example, no indigenous large ungulates in Australia and therefore no scavengers to dispose of their dung. But when man eventually introduced six million cattle, each of which dropped twelve pats of dung a day and covered one-tenth of an acre every year with hardened pats that could survive intact for several years in the absence of scavengers, vast areas of good pasture became pocked with rank growths of coarse, mainly inedible grass; moreover, the deposits of dung also provided breeding grounds for an astronomical population of flies. Since 1967, therefore, attempts have been made to introduce dung beetles to Australia. Initially these appeared to be successful, until the giant toads, imported from South America some thirty years earlier to control the sugarcane beetle, began to prey on the dung beetles. Australian ecologists must now, therefore, experiment with the giant armored species of dung beetles, which might repel the toads, or with diurnal species, which might escape the attention of the nocturnal toads, though not perhaps those of any birds that might be attracted by them.

The African savannas are so renowned for their colossal aggregations of game and spectacular predators that their vast bird population tends to be overshadowed. Yet they are the habitat of multitudes of seed- and insect-eating birds, breeding in colonies of millions. The most numerous of these are the weaverbirds and, in particular, the sparrow-sized quelea or red-billed dioch, whose estimated population of 100,000 million may become as great a scourge to man's crops as were the locusts, and have serious effects on the economies of twenty-five African countries in which food is scarce under the most favorable conditions, for although 90 percent of the adult queleas' food consists of the seeds of wild grasses, they also devastate crops of rice, millet, wheat, and maize, migrating up to 1000 miles in search of these "granaries."

Most weaverbirds depend upon grasses not only for food, but also for building material with which to construct their intricately woven nests. Most are polygamous, with the cocks building several nests and defending territories containing a number of hens. With the coming of the rains, millions of pairs of queleas assemble in breeding colonies, concentrated perhaps in 4 square miles of dense thornbush and acacia; and although they do not, like the social weaverbirds of southwest Africa, cooperate in building gigantic communal nest structures housing as many as three hundred pairs, a single tree may hold four hundred quelea nests. Their numbers are too great to be controlled by predators or, apparently, by man, despite the destruction of roosts of ten or twenty-five million birds covering as much as 40 square miles, for each pair of queleas can breed three or four times in a single season, and rear almost 90 percent of the full complement of nine or twelve nestlings. They are, however, vulnerable to drought, for they can only construct their nests if there has been sufficient rain to produce green grass with stems and blades long enough for the males to weave and, subsequently, seeds and insects with which to feed the young. If the rains fail they do not breed.

The African savannas also provide ideal hunting and feeding grounds for a larger population of avian raptors and scavengers than any other region in the world. Together with the carnivores, they maintain a constant pressure on the smaller prey species. Many are specialist snake-eaters, bird catchers, mammal hunters, or insectivores. Secretary birds kill snakes, striking viciously with their strong clawed feet beneath the dark shields of their spread wings; marabou storks hunt rodents and reptiles along the fringes of grass fires, and also compete with vultures at carrion. As a contributor to *The Living World of Animals* has pointed out, the vultures' long, broad, and deeply slotted wings enable them not only to soar easily on columns of rising air and gain height rapidly on strong currents, as they maneuver in tight circles, but also to fly slowly without stalling in still air, dropping only 1 or 3 feet.

Felix Rodriquez de la Fuente has described in *Hunters and Hunted of the Savannah,* how:

As soon as the sun begins to warm the air of the savannah— about two hours after it has risen—the vultures, which until then have remained perched on the branches of the acacias or on rocky outcrops . . . allow themselves to be borne upwards on the thermal currents and soon manage to reach a considerable height—sometimes as much as 7,000 feet. Around midmorning the sky may be darkened by glider-like forms as the birds soar and swoop above the open plains. . . . The moment one of them spots an animal's dead body and dives straight downwards to investigate, the birds in the vicinity immediately follow suit, legs outstretched and wings flapping violently.

Individuals of five or six species of vultures (most of which also inhabit scrub and desert regions) may be included in an assembly of a hundred at a single carcass or abandoned kill, and may have gathered to it—one sighting the plunging form of another—from 70 miles around. Often, however, they have time only to rip away a beakful or two because their alighting has been observed and acted upon by terrestrial carnivores such as hyenas or jackals, or even lions, which are alerted by the whistling of the air through a plummeting vulture's wing feathers. Hyenas will gallop miles at the sight of a vulture stooping or of white storks alighting; conversely, vultures are attracted by tape recordings of hyenas at a kill. Hyenas utter an extraordinary variety of sounds, of which the most frequently employed, as a contact call, is a weird whooping *oooo-whup*, included in a series of ten or more calls that begin loudly and often terminate in a very soft, low, single-syllable *oooo*. Their giggles, yells, and growls at a kill attract other hyenas from great distances, and also lions.

When the wildebeest are calving, their placentas provide the savanna jackals with their main source of food, and Jane van Lawick-Goodall has described how a pair of these jackals would suddenly become alert, staring up at the tiny shape of a vulture

plummeting down from a great height. As soon as they had ascertained in which direction the bird was descending, they
would streak across the plain, often arriving only seconds after
the vulture had alighted, and appropriate the great part of the
afterbirth. Black-backed jackals may assemble in large numbers
at a carcass, with as many as seventeen darting in and out to
seize scraps from the kill of a tolerant lion.

The vultures cannot begin feeding until the carnivores have
had their fill, though they can drive off jackals by weight of
numbers, but despite the apparent confusion among the scores
of vultures scrimmaging over and within a carcass, competition
is largely avoided because the individuals of the different species
feed on different parts of the carcass. The powerful lappet-faced
and white-headed vultures open up the tough hide and cut the
tendons with their strong beaks; the griffons and white-backed
vultures, with hygienically unfeathered necks, tackle the intes-
tines and soft muscles with long beaks and rasplike tongues;
while the narrow-beaked Egyptian and hooded vultures pick up
the scraps strewn around by the others—until all the carcass except the bones has been rapidly consumed.

The Egyptian vultures are of particular interest because they
are the only animals that have developed a special stone-throwing technique for opening the ostrichs' enormous eggs, 6 or 8
inches long and 3 pounds in weight, in order to extract their
contents, though in Bushman Land, where ostriches are especially numerous, the pied crows carry stones to a height and
drop them on nests of ostrich eggs. However, according to Jane
van Lawick-Goodall, the sight of an ostrich egg, even when it is
several hundred yards away, so stimulates Egyptian vultures
that they usually pick up stones and throw them at the ground
while they move toward the proper target: "On some occasions
when one dominant vulture chases away a subordinate, the lat-

The Egyptian vulture

ter, frustrated in its attempt to get at the egg, usually walks round throwing stone after stone at the ground!"

Normally, half a dozen or a dozen directs hits with a stone are sufficient to crack the shell, though it is thick enough to resist the heat of a savanna fire. One of a pair of vultures at a deserted nest, containing fifteen whole eggs and half a dozen broken ones, threw stones repeatedly at an egg for four minutes until the shell cracked and the yolk oozed through. That they are extraordinarily persistent is illustrated by another pair, which bombarded an experimental fiber-glass egg for one and a half hours until it was finally removed.

Their technique is described by Jane van Lawick-Goodall in an article in *Animals:*

> The stone is thrown with a forceful downward movement of head and neck during which the missile is released from the beak. Usually a bird scores an approximately equal number of hits and misses during the performance, but on the rare occasions when two birds work together the throwing tends to be rather more wild. One bird, in fact, twice hit its companion instead of the egg! Sometimes when there are no suitable stones near the egg the vultures search the ground for distances of up to 50 yards, often picking up but discarding tiny pebbles, and sometimes trying desperately to raise heavy rocks in their beaks. The average weight of stones actually thrown during our tests was 5 ounces, but once a vulture managed to lift and throw a rock weighing over 2 pounds—a fantastic performance for a slender-beaked bird no bigger than a raven.

She concluded that this stone-throwing technique is stimulated by the shape of the ostrich's egg, for, under experimental conditions, a vulture would pick and throw stones not only at giant fiber-glass eggs, but at ostrich eggs painted different colors and also at slightly smaller eggs too large to be picked up in its beak, whereas a cube, though approximately the same size and color as an ostrich's egg, was totally ignored. It is interesting to learn that two captive banded mongooses, which in the wild state habitually open small eggs by throwing them between their legs against a rock, initially attempted to tackle an ostrich's egg in this way, but, not being successful they threw stones between their legs at the egg. Ostrich eggs present no problem to the powerfully jawed hyenas, which eat large numbers of them and also the young birds, while jackals are reputed to butt the eggs against each other until they break.

Ostriches are still common in many parts of Africa, including not only the open grasslands and savannas, but also arid thorn-bush country and semidesert, for they range into the Sahara and Libyan deserts, where Ralph Bagnold encountered them in flocks of fifty or a hundred, grazing in company with large numbers of oryx in the more vegetated southern regions, during the course of a number of expeditions between 1927 and 1932. They also formerly inhabited the Syrian and Arabian deserts, where one was found dying in floodwater in Jordan as recently as 1966. They have survived because they can outrun most predators, covering the ground with 12- or 15-foot strides at speeds of up to 45 miles per hour over long distances. They are also most formidable opponents—sharing with rhinos the repu-tation of charging trains—for, as Eve Palmer notes in her de-lightful book, *The Plains of Camdeboo*, their "immense dinosaur legs kick with ferocious power, sending a man spinning, and the frightful two-toed, two-clawed feet rip flesh from bones with ease. Sometimes an ostrich will kneel and roll upon a prostrate body, scrunching the bones as it does so." Thus a kick from this huge bird, weighing between 165 and 330 pounds, is sufficient to deter all but the strongest and hungriest predators, and even lions apparently seldom kill them though using their eggs as playthings if they can drive the parent birds away from the nest. Anthony Cullen has indeed described one lion rolling over with an egg clasped to his stomach. However, none of the eggs in this nest were broken and more than half of them subsequently hatched after being replaced in the nest.

Rival cocks, however, sometimes fight, inflicting deep wounds, although serious injury is usually avoided because they are protected, both from kicks and from the heat of the sand when they are crouching, by the flat shield that replaced the distinctive breastbone keel to which the muscles of a flying bird are attached, and which is so thick and strong that an eighteen-month-old ostrich was seen to break through a stone wall 2 feet thick by running against it.

Ostriches are generally stated to be polygamous, calling up half a dozen hens during the mating season with repeated "roarings" of two short deep booms followed by one long one, with neck partially inflated and beak closed. Various observers, including S. C. Cronwright-Schreiner—who was born on the veld in 1863 and had an ostrich farm on the mid-Karoo in Cape Province, but is perhaps better known vicariously as the husband of Olive Schreiner, author of *An African Farm*—have described how during the day, when territorial jealousies apparently lapse and a number of cocks and hens are feeding together, one cock will suddenly bump down on his knees in front of a hen, extend his wings and swing them alternately backward and forward, each wing as it comes forward being raised while that going backward is depressed. Every feather of his plumage is erected and the white plumes at the ends of the wings are alternately and rhythmically spread like a fan and closed. His neck is lowered until his head is aligned with his back, and as head and neck swing from side to side, the back of the head strikes with a loud click against the wings, first on one side and then on the other, while the tail is fluttered rapidly up and down. After "rolling" or displaying in this manner for ten minutes or so—which he will also do at intervals when chasing a man on horseback, hissing viciously—the cock rises and makes a short stamping rush toward the hen, before dropping down on his knees again and displaying even more fervently. Totally involved in his ritual, this is the one time when an ostrich is vulnerable to attack.

The actual nest site is a trampled area about 10 feet in diameter, in which the grass has been plucked up by the roots or grazed down, and the soil or sand scratched up. Here, in a shallow depression, 1 foot deep and 3 feet across, a number of hens lay from three to a dozen eggs each every other day, with the result that one nest may contain as many as ninety-four eggs. But when their clutches are complete, all but one of the hens leave the site, and responsibility for the six or seven weeks' incubation and the rearing of the chicks devolves upon the cock and the remaining hen. Although it is usually stated that the cock incubates by night, when his black and white plumage is less conspicuous, and the brownish hen by day, this may be another of the generalizations about ostrich behavior—which has been little studied. Cronwright-Schreiner was quite definite that cock and hen incubated alternately for some hours at a time around the clock, both sitting tightly except when leaving the nest to entice a predator away with the familiar "broken-wing" antic. David Sheldrick, when director of the Tsavo National Park, saw one cock continuing to sit on its eggs although engulfed in the flames of a very large bush fire. By laying its head close to the ground and fanning its feathers, while the flames swept over it, it escaped unharmed.

Cronwright-Schreiner also considered that ostriches were not truly polygamous, because in his experience a pair whose nest was laid in by other hens frequently abandoned it, while although several hens might lay in one nest, this actually resulted in fewer chicks hatching because of the disturbance and breakage among the eggs caused by more than one hen attempting to incubate. A sitting ostrich is often surrounded by conspicuous white eggs which, in Cronwright-Schreiner's experience, had rolled out of the nest or had been displaced by the activities of a number of hens. More recent observers claim that, since the eggs are laid at intervals by the various hens, some are being incubated before others have been laid, and that toward the end of the incubation period, the parents remove the first eggs laid, when the embryos have reached a certain stage of development, and deposit them in hollows at a little distance from the nest, where their incubation is completed by the heat of the sun.

Once hatched, the 12-inch chicks are able to run swiftly as soon as they have dried off, and to feed on small legumes and weeds, and at a later stage apparently amalgamate with other broods, for George Adamson records seeing a pair of adults with more than fifty half-grown young, while Joy Adamson photographed a cock leading more than a hundred well-grown young; and Cullen has a record of a cock and hen with 285 chicks in February, of which 265 were still alive the following September. Although the chicks are fully grown when a year old, they do not breed until four or five years old.

12: Large and Small Game on the Savannas

A feature of the enormous aggregations of animals grazing on the savannas is the intermingling of different species, including not only antelopes, gazelles, and zebras, but also with them giraffes, and ostriches in flocks of half a dozen or thirty. Each species contributes to a communal defense against predators. Cock ostriches stand 8 feet, the hens slightly less, and their keen dark eyes (protected from dust by lids fringed with thick hair) and lofty stature, like that of the 18-foot bull and 15-foot cow giraffes, supplement the acute noses of the zebras and the alertness of the antelope and gazelles. Some species often associate with hartebeest, which habitually post sentinels, and when a mixed herd of wildebeest and zebra are resting, three or four of the former station themselves on an old termite mound, facing in different directions in order to cover the maximum field of view.

Ostriches are also ever on the *qui vive*, never sleeping for longer than a quarter of an hour at a time; and they must indeed be considered as avian ungulates, belonging to the same group as the larger herbivores, though in addition to grasses, cereals, thistles, berries, and fruits, they also feed on rats, grasshoppers, lizards, snakes, and young tortoises. Antelope do not sleep deeply for longer than four minutes, nor zebra for more than ten minutes during the hours of daylight. Even when resting or ruminating, an antelope remains alert to the stimulus of danger, and rarely are all the individuals in a herd asleep at the same time. They sit with their backs to the wind, heads up and legs stretched out or tucked under their bellies, but seldom lying on their sides in a position that upsets their complicated digestive systems.

When alarmed small antelopes and gazelles, and even their fawns, employ an antic known as "pronking" in the case of the springboks, in which they buck like rodeo mustangs with backs sharply arched and haunches down, legs hanging fully extended and hooves nearly bunched together, and heads lowered almost to the feet, while bounding stiff-legged, as if on springs, 8 or 10 feet into the air several times in quick succession. When a Thomson's gazelle (or Tommy) pronks, the contraction of the skin on its flanks ripples the vivid black lateral stripe that outlines its white underparts, and when a Grant's gazelle does so, the white hairs of its black-bordered rump patch flare. In either case a warning signal is emitted to other individuals in the vicinity. But the supreme exponent of pronking is the springbok, which is adorned from midback to rump with a crest or fan of long hairs—the outer ones brown, the inner and longer ones white—that normally lie flat. Cronwright-Schreiner, in *The Migratory Springboks of South Africa,* has described a springbok pronking:

In an instant the buck seems to spurn the earth as it shoots up into the air to an incredible height, perhaps straight up; for an instant it hangs arched, then down it drops. . . . The buck seems scarcely to touch the earth when it bounds up into the air again like a rocket . . . for a second you see it in the air, its mane up, its fan raised and opened in a sharp arch, the white patch blazing in the sun and the long hairs glittering . . . then it touches earth again, only to bound up once more at a sharp angle to one side, then straighten up, then to the other side, then forward. . . . Then it will pronk away straight on end, with prodigious leaps, until eventually it will set off at full speed with the fan down.

One springbok pronking sets off others, "heliographing" immense distances over the veld, and, wrote the big game hunter, Roualeyn Gordon-Cumming, in *The Lion of South Africa*, "away start the herd with a succession of strange perpendicular bounds, rising with curved loins high into the air, and at the same time elevating the snowy folds of long white hair on their haunches and along their back. . . . They bound to the height of ten or twelve feet, with the elasticity of an india-rubber ball, clearing at each spring from twelve to fifteen feet of ground, without apparently the slightest exertion. In performing this spring they appear for an instant as if suspended in the air, when down come all four feet again together, and, striking the plain, away they soar again, as if about to take flight. The herd only adopt this motion for a few hundred yards, when they subside into a light elastic trot, arching their graceful necks and lowering their noses to the ground."

When the veld is warmed by the winter sun and snow is in the air, the springboks pronk for the joy of it, vaulting over each other's backs; and Eve Palmer has described how, "drinking the wind as they fly, racing and bounding in their flight, they are one moment part of the veld and the next they are part of the sky . . . as if the veld they trod was a giant trampoline. . . . And as they bucked and bounded they flaunted their white fans, the long snowy gossamer hairs upon their backs."

Within the loosely knit assemblies of the different species of game herding on the savannas, the lives of many are dominated by strict territorial rules governing both feeding and sexual behavior. As Rennie Bere has pointed out, in an article in *Animals*, a first impression of a herd of a few hundred of the stocky red kob is of antelope scattered widely and at random over the grasslands or lightly wooded savanna. Most are grazing, some resting and cudding, "others weaving in and out of the groups at a fast and purposeful gallop. Even so, none of them go far away or

A springbok pronking

cross what seems to be an invisible line . . . this is the limit held corporately by the herd."

In fact the herd comprises several clearly defined groups and from a dozen to forty solitary individuals. Three or four of the groups, each of which may include as many as a hundred members, are composed exclusively of males over the age of eight or nine months; the other groups, fifteen or twenty strong, are does and juveniles; and there are solitaries, adult bucks, each of which occupies a territory 20 to 40 yards in diameter over an area of short grass. Where kob are numerous, these male territories may almost overlap, but though the bucks may engage in trials of strength with interlocked horns, there are no vicious combats. In many cases their territories, some of which are known to have been identical for at least thirty years, are centered around termite mounds and include a resting place, trampled flat and almost denuded of grass, and a defecating place.

The does, which come into season in any month of the year, resort to the bucks' territorial area to mate with a number of them, not necessarily the largest though usually the most active, and then return to their female group. Thus, a buck cannot mate unless he owns a territory, and, to ensure that he is not supplanted by another buck, he constantly patrols its bounds, demarcating these by dragging his hooves and thereby depositing scent from glands on his feet. He grazes as closely as possible to his mound and hurries back to it from brief visits to water hole or salt lick. Territorial bucks are drawn from the reserve groups of bachelors, and if one loses his territory to a rival, he returns to his bachelor group.

The key to the teeming life of the African savannas is their highly nutritious and tenacious grasses, notably the saw-toothed grass, only 5 or 6 inches high, which thrives on close cropping by many kinds of herbivores, and the dominant red oat grass which, when it flowers, transforms the plains into a russet sea. Its seeds can lie dormant beneath a charred layer of soil, and its fresh, fire-induced shoots are, like those of star grass, a richer source of protein, calcium, and phosphorus than the taller older growths. Thus the savannas of East Africa in particular can support the most spectacular concentrations of game remaining on earth, including more than forty large species, of which as many as sixteen may be in one grazing assemblage. A single herd of migrating wildebeest or zebra may be ten thousand strong, but even so the total numbers of the smaller herds of antelope and gazelles far outnumber them.

It is only in recent years that research in the field by several zoologists and their teams on the now famous Serengeti plains has enabled us to form some conception of the approximate numbers of animals involved in these concentrations of game on the savannas, though these are so great and are likely to fluctuate so drastically between research periods that estimates tend to "yo-yo" wildly from one count to the next. Twenty-five species of ungulates, in addition to giraffes, rhino, elephants, and the predators large and small, live on the Serengeti plains, which slope gently and irregularly from an altitude of some 6000 feet in the east near the Rift Valley to about 4000 feet near the shores of Lake Victoria.

In 1972 the ungulates included an estimated 750,000 wildebeest, whose numbers have more than doubled during the past decade; between 600,000 and 950,000 Thomson's gazelles, and from 60,000 to 100,000 Grant's gazelles; 65,000 or 70,000 impala; 25,000 topi and 18,000 kongoni—both hartebeests; 7000 eland; 50,000 buffalo, which have trebled in numbers during the past decade; together with upward of 200,000 zebra, 8000 giraffes, 15,000 warthogs, 5000 ostriches, and 13,000 "others," adding up to the stupendous total of around 2 million herbivores grazing, browsing, and rooting at certain seasons of the year over the Serengeti's total area of 15,000 square miles.

Yet, by and large, there is apparently no significant competition for forage among the different species, because all have their particular vegetational niches and preferences. They graze on different kinds of grasses, browse on shrubs at different heights, or, when a number of species feed on the same plant, crop it at different stages of its growth, with the result that their use of the plant is complementary not competitive. Where the concentration of game is heavy, there tends to be a regular grazing sequence, with the zebra usually in the van, because their possession of upper incisors enables them to tackle coarser growths than antelope or cattle. Thus, while zebra, wildebeest, and topi all graze the red oat grass, the zebra do so when it is mature with tough stems, whereas the wildebeest prefer the young green leaves and stems, cropping the horizontal leaves until the grass is about 4 inches high, while the topi reject it when it is green but crop the withered lower parts of the stems. Several days later, when new grass sprouts from the cropped base, the small, 50-pound Tommies nibble at this fresh growth with their slender muzzles, though they prefer the green leaves of star grass and the many nutritious herbs among the grasses.

Buffalo, grazing in closer order than the antelope and zebras, play their part in maintaining the pasture in good heart, for, as Jane Burton has described in *Animals of the African Year*, "Nosing beneath the tough top growth, they bite off the lusher softer green shoots below, trampling the residue into a mulch. . . . Patches of long grass which the buffalo miss, either because it is unpalatable or has snags of fallen branches among it . . . in times of drought act as a useful reserve of standing hay."

The grasses are not of course the only source of food on the savannas. The Tommies' larger relatives, the 150-pound Grant's gazelles, feed mainly on herbs and shrubs, browsing on leaves and twigs. The tiny dik-diks, only 12 inches high at the shoulder, feed on the lowest growth of shrubs, though changing to grass when seasonally available and thus making the fullest use of an arid habitat. The 1800-pound giant eland both grazes and browses shrubs and the lower leaves and twigs of trees; while the fantastically long-necked gerenuk gazelles with, in Evelyn Ames's words, "hooves like the feet and slippers of ballet dancers" and, more prosaically, an unusual adaptation of the hip joint, can utilize another food source by standing upright for long periods on their slender hind legs, with their forefeet among the branches, while plucking delicacies off the tops of small bushes and browsing acacias to a height of about 54 inches.

Finally, the giraffes can exploit the upper parts of trees that are not accessible to any other herbivores, if one excepts elephants which push the trees over. Almost 90 percent of the giraffes' food consists of leaves, which they grip and pluck with their sticky, 18-inch tongues, without thrusting their muzzles among the thorns. In summer about half the hours of daylight, and in spring, when not many trees are in leaf, three-quarters are spent in browsing. Foraging in groups of two or three or exceptionally fifty over 20 miles or more of acacia-studded savanna and thornbush country, and even into waterless desert, up to an altitude of 8000 feet, the giraffes crop the trees in some districts so heavily that they have "browse-lined" their contours between 3½ feet and 17 feet above the ground. Some they dwarf by ripping off the tips of 4-foot saplings; gardenias are pruned to the shapes of conical flasks, and torchwoods into hourglasses; desert dates are reduced to impenetrable tangles of 2-inch spikes at the center; and umbrella trees—so characteristic of the savannas—are stripped of all foliage below their unreachable flat-topped

crowns, whose ribs, in Evelyn Ames's words again, "flare upwards in a single layer of lace against the sky from which
hang—on one side of the tree only—the round gold balls of the
weaverbirds' nests." For 40 or 60 or even 120 feet across their
crowns, the umbrella trees draw into the circle of their heavy
shade, where the grass grows shoulder-high, large herds of gazelles—rangy fawn and white Grant's with long spiraling horns,
and golden-russet Tommies incessantly flicking their tails.
When a tail stops wagging, neighbors take notice of possible
danger, and a newborn Tommy can wag its tail before it can
move its legs.

Though browsing on a variety of trees, giraffes prefer acacias,
including the miniature whistling thorns or ant galls that dot the
savannas and might well overwhelm them if not kept in check
by the regular grass fires. Most acacias bear formidable hooked
thorns of spikes which, however, are soft and palatable when
growing; but in addition to their hard, double-forked, silvery
spikes, an inch or two long, the whistling thorns are also "protected" by colonies of painfully biting, small, black Crematoga-
ster ants that live in the hollow, acorn-like gall that develops at
the base of each pair of spikes. Initially these galls, hanging in
paired black baubles from twigs and branches, are soft and bear
leaves, but as they dry they harden and blacken, the leaves are
shed, and the ants take possession of them with each gall housing a self-contained colony, though there is reported to be only
one queen to a tree. The ants scurry in and out of the minute
round holes in the galls, and the wind, vibrating the spines and
rushing into the thousands of holes, is responsible for the per-
petual whistling or moaning associated with these acacias and
amplified by the hollow interior of the galls.

It is generally suggested, as a neat ecological package, that the
spikes protect the ants' nests from predators, while the ants

repel insects that might damage the trees' foliage (whose dense covert attracts the tsetse fly), and that would-be browsers such as impala are deterred by the combination of spikes and of ants swarming onto and biting their muzzles. In fact baboons show no hesitation in picking the galls and munching them for the insect food they contain, spitting out the hard vegetable parts; giraffes, whose mouth linings are protected by saliva as thick as a rubber solution, take the spikes between their soft lips and grind them up with their molars; while black rhinos, plucking them with their upper lips which terminate in a finger-like point, may eat more than 250 galls in a day. Even acacia rats, though they do not apparently feed either on the ants or the young galls, build very large dreylike nests of living twigs on the tops of capacious old whistling thorns.

Black rhinos display an extraordinary liking for thorny acacias, despite the fact that their spikes are tough enough to penetrate the tires of cars, and thrive on coarser forms of vegetation than most other herbivores, though they are known to feed on at least 190 varieties of shrubs, legumes, and herbs, sampling as many as 100 different ones in the course of a day's browsing, whereas the square-lipped white rhino is exclusively a grazer of grass and, like the hippo, possesses a strip of cartilage in the lower lip which enables it to crop very closely. Included in the black rhino's forage are several plants that are highly toxic to other herbivores. These are eaten more particularly in arid country and during the dry season when the rhinos are especially selective in their choice of food in order to obtain moisture from the greener parts of plants. In these conditions they frequently chew the skulls of wildebeest—to make good, no doubt, mineral deficiencies—and eat their dried dung, chewing a mouthful for several minutes before swallowing a portion. They also sample thorn apples and such latex-bearing plants as euphorbias and wild sisal, from which elephants and lions extract moisture.

Some euphorbias trail along the ground, others grow to trees, 15 or 20 feet tall, with smooth, rubbery green leaves. Their milk-white latex sap is bitter to the taste, and the rhinos masticate the leaf stems for twenty minutes or more before spitting out the fibers. According to Jane Burton finger euphorbia in particular is eaten in large quantities, and in order to get at high branches a rhino will incongruously rear up on its hind legs and reach up as far as it can with its front feet, then hook its horns among the branches and, walking backward, snap off large portions of the tree, eating all the smaller branches and gouging the bark off with its teeth and curved front horn. That so many rhinos have the front horn broken or missing may perhaps be attributed to these arboreal activities rather than to combat. Since finger euphorbia is not indigenous to East Africa, but was introduced from India, one wonders what effect its widespread colonization has had on the distribution of black rhinos in arid waterless regions.

Rhinos are reputed never to venture outside their home range and, if this does not contain permanent water, to thirst rather than undertake long treks in search of water, but when possible they drink and wallow every day, though if their water holes dry out, they may have to trek 5 or 10 miles to a dry riverbed and dig down 3 feet to a seepage. Although essentially solitary beasts, as many as a dozen may gather at a wallow for a couple of hours before sunset, to roll over on their sides and plaster themselves with mud, thereby dissipating excess heat accumulated during the day and armoring themselves against biting flies. If muddy wallows are not to be found during droughts, they "dust" in the fine-grained soil provided by termite hills.

Their main period of activity is between dusk and dawn, and

after their early morning feed, when their slow rhythmic chewing, champing of twigs, and cracking of branches are plainly audible for distances of 50 yards or more, they retreat to the shade of a tree or just as often to a dust bowl exposed to the full heat of the sun. There they may rest and doze for ten hours at a stretch, though always responsive to the activities of the red-billed and yellow-billed oxpecker birds, whose warning calls may "compensate" rhinos for their exceptional shortsightedness, though this is offset to some degree by their acute sense of smell and fair hearing. But every one and a quarter hours or so resting rhinos must get to their feet for a ten-minute walkabout, in order to avoid crushing the radial nerve and becoming temporarily paralyzed. And ultimately, when it becomes cooler, they rouse themselves and wander off alone or in twos or threes to feed.

The size of a rhino's home range, demarcated by short puffs or sprays of urine as the owner ambles along feeding, naturally varies according to the availability of food and water. A square mile of dense bush and yellow-barked acacias or fever trees may hold sufficient food (and also covert) throughout the year for more than a score of rhinos, whereas where vegetation is less abundant and water holes fewer, each rhino may require 6 or 12 miles. A juvenile's tract is nearly twice the size of an adult's, because when it is driven away by its mother on the birth of a new calf and joins up with another juvenile or with an adult female, it is still allowed to feed on its mother's ground, while at the same time having the freedom of its new companion's range.

There is no consensus of opinion as to whether or not rhinos claim definite territories. In the arid country of the Tsavo National Park East (on the marches between Kenya and Tanzania), where the rhinos' browsing range extends for many miles away from sources of permanent water, they are nomadic in a limited sense, with several different rhinos sharing in common feeding grounds, sleeping places, wallows, tracks, and water holes. Certainly, all adult "territories" overlap considerably, and normally neither owner is aggressive when two meet, while intruders from more distant ranges usually retreat when threatened physically or vocally. However, although when two cow rhinos meet they, according to George W. Frame, "normally nudge one another gently with their horns or with the sides of the head, and thereafter show indifference to the other's presence," a bull has been known to kill a strange cow and her calf straying onto its range. Rhinos are both polygynous and polyandrous, and Frame describes in an article in *Animals* how when a bull meets a cow one or both emit characteristic puffing snorts:

> Then the male approaches the female with short cautious steps, occasionally thrashing his head from side to side in a sweeping motion or jabbing the air with his front horn. When the female charges, the male wheels around and gallops in a tight circle, only to return to her with the cautious short-step approach. . . . This may continue for several hours, or until one of them walks away.

These antediluvian colossi, weighing a ton or more, yet so gentle and affectionate when hand-fed from birth, are not significantly affected by natural predators, though lions and hunting dogs kill some calves, and hyenas attempt to hamstring them, but are usually successfully driven off by the cows. In Kenya in particular there have also been several instances of encounters between cow elephants and cow rhinos, most of which have resulted in the elephant killing both cow and calf, and almost invariably covering their carcasses with branches and brush. However, both black and white rhinos have a low breeding rate, producing only one calf every three years or so, and because of their sedentary habits do not colonize depopulated areas. Local populations are therefore always at risk from poachers and from the encroachment on their habitat by the ever-increasing native peoples. The white rhino in particular does not readily adapt to changes in environment or forage, and is now reduced to a total African population of some two thousand the majority of which are located in national parks.

No animal has had such a profound effect on the environment and ecology of the savannas as the bush elephant, with his immense strength and gargantuan appetite. Although elephants may create new woodlands by, for example, eating the fruits of Borassus palms and subsequently evacuating their iron-hard seeds in their droppings in other places several miles distant, their more usual role is that of converting large tracts of land from dense bush into open woodlands. A large herd of elephants feeding in an isolated block of hardwood or dry thornbush damage and also kill the trees by browsing, ringbarking, and pushing them over, while by trampling the shrubbery they let in light, which encourages the growth of grasses and allows the seasonal grass fires to sweep through the accumulation of dead timber and branches and destroy and seedling regeneration. Thus bush and woodland are ultimately transformed into treeless savanna.

On the other hand Daphne Sheldrick believes the elephant to be the ecological key to the 8000 square miles of the eastern section of the Tsavo National Park, stating in *The Tsavo Story* that:

Almost every animal in Tsavo is dependent on the elephant in some form or another; many even for their food. . . . Were the elephant not there to trample and crop the grass when it becomes rank in the wet season, keeping it short and palatable for the grazing animals, they . . . would suffer. . . . They also play a vital role in the provision of water. By puddling with their great feet the depressions that trap rain-water in the wet season, they seal the soil and make it impervious. They create new water-holes by rolling and bathing in these puddles, plastering large amounts of mud on their enormous bodies. . . . By trampling they can even raise the water table in watercourses, causing underground water to flow on the surface.

The bulls and old cows are the main well diggers, and in the most intimate account of elephants yet published, Ian and Oria Douglas-Hamilton have described in *Among the Elephants* how, using their feet as shovels to loosen the soil, they would kick the sand backward and forward until a wide hole had been formed:

> At times they would dig down three feet or more with their trunks and feet, their toenails acting like a spade. They would push this sand with a side of a foot onto the curved end of the trunk, which they used like a cupped hand to throw the sand to one side. When the sand got damp and the water began to seep into the hole, they tensed the lips of their trunks, like fingers, to dig a deep, narrow, clean hole. The muddy water was rapidly picked up and spewed around in circles or blown out like a suction pump and with the same noise. It was amazing how professional they were at the job. Within about a quarter of an hour little wells had been dug all over the place, some only a few feet away from each other.

Elephants also excavate holes with their tusks deep enough to avoid filling their trunks with sand when they drink. Nevertheless in drought years, when all food is scarce and competition for that available is intense, they can be the cause of a heavy mortality among other animals. Bush elephants are the most adaptable of all large herbivores in their diet, feeding in a hundred different items, from coarse head-high grasses rejected by other herbivores to bulbs and tubers which they grub up with tusks and feet, while in the dry season they subsist mainly on the bark and twigs of trees and bushes near rivers or perma-

Bush elephant

nent water holes, stripping the tough bark off thorn trees with their tusks and whittling the bark off twigs between their teeth. In *Return to the Wild*, Norman Carr has described a herd feeding during the winter in the Zambian valley of the Luangwa, where the river is flanked by parklike country dominated by the majestic winter thorn, whose pods resembling fried apple rings are highly nutritious, and by tamarinds and sausage trees with gigantic sausage-shaped fruits suspended on long, cordlike stalks:

> Elephants could be seen throughout the day in the glades between the shady trees on both sides of the river grazing on the mlanje grass which they uprooted with their trunks, knocking the earth off by smacking the roots on their foreheads or chests. When they were not eating grass they would tear down the Bohenia trees to get at the pods. . . . But the elephants' favourite relish at this time of the year is the seed from the Winter Thorn. . . . Although a fully grown tree is half as large again as a giant oak. . . . A large bull will lift up his trunk and lay it perpendicularly against the tree and with all his six tons behind him shake until the tree shudders and rains down seeds. He and the lesser members of the group will then pick up each curly pod meticulously with the tips of their trunks and transfer them to their mouths.

He goes on to describe in *The White Impala* how if the tree is too massive to shake, an elephant will stretch up its trunk and tear down one of the lower branches to get at the pods: "In well-used elephant country very few of these lower limbs remain, so it has to stand on its back legs, lifting its forefeet and extending its trunk perpendicularly to reach up to a phenomenal height . . . in order to reach the nearest branch. I have actually measured the reach of an elephant stretching up in this way. It extended for more than twenty-four feet."

Since its digestive system is not very efficient, an elephant must forage almost continuously to maintain its strength, and may indeed feed for nineteen and a half hours out of the twenty-four, while sampling as many as sixty-four different kinds of vegetation, but because much of its food is woody or fibrous, it is likely to starve in extreme drought conditions, not primarily from the lack of available food, but because of the absence of proteins in it. Daphne Sheldrick has described the curious behavior of elephants during a drought in the Tsavo Park, where exceptionally severe droughts occur approximately every ten years. About 1956, some years before this particular drought, the elephants began to behave very strangely during the normal dry season, pushing over great tracts of the gnarled and twisted crab-apple-like commiphora trees with flaking papery bark of many shades of reds and greens and pure robin's-egg blue, yet frequently eating very little or nothing at all of the trees after they had felled them. Moreover, during the following season of 1957, when food and water were abundant, they continued felling the commiphoras as if, wrote Daphne Sheldrick, pursuing a deliberate act of policy, transforming the park into a lunar landscape of desolation.

It was about this time Carr reported that elephants in the Luangwa valley, a thousand miles to the south, had begun to attack baobab trees, whereas previously they had never been observed to feed on them in that region, though all parts of these weird trees—branches, leaves, the great waxy flowers that bloom for a single day, and the pulp and seeds of the hard-shelled fruits—are in fact eaten by many animals, including elephants, which rip the huge boles apart in order to obtain calcium or water. Although a thick bark conserves the moisture in the baobab's woody tissue, the latter is so soft that a bullet can travel right through the bole, and Carr describes how toward the end of the dry season hardly a tree remained that had not been mutilated by the elephants:

> Tirelessly they teaze away at the soft fibrous tree with their tusks and pull off the loosened fibres with their trunks, returning day after day to the same tree until they have excavated a huge cavity in the massive trunk.

He suggests that an increase in the number of elephants, coupled with the contraction of their habitat and choice of forage,
may have resulted in a deficiency of calcium and other minerals;
and he adds that at least a dozen species of trees and plants have
been depleted in the Luangwa due to increases in the populations of a number of herbivores. In the twenty years since Carr's
experiences, the elephant population in the Luangwa watershed
has increased enormously, possibly to a hundred thousand, and
is causing extensive damage to the baobabs and winter-thorns.
Once again the conservationist is confronted by his occupational
nightmare of whether to allow the elephants to work out their
own destiny by temporarily destroying their habitat, or whether
their numbers should be reduced by "cropping" before this stage
has been reached.

But, to return to Tsavo. In 1960–61 came the very severe
drought when three hundred rhinos starved to death along a 40-
mile stretch of the Athi River, because they characteristically
would not migrate out of their home range to new feeding
grounds. Elephants normally browse the bush down to a level of
from 4 to 6 feet above the ground, while rhino browse in the 1-
to 3-foot layer, though on the plains of the Serengeti and the
Ngorongoro Crater, they also feed on very low-growing plants.
Where elephants, then, are trampling down the vegetation in
large herds, the rhinos are restricted to foraging on what the elephants neglect.

It was generally expected that the elephants' long-term systematic destruction of the commiphora trees would result in
desert conditions prevailing in the park thereafter. But as we
have seen, to Daphne Sheldrick their behavior gave the impression of being a deliberate act of policy, and the remarkable fact
is that when the 1961 drought was followed by six years of normal rainfall, fresh springs of water appeared, seedling acacias re-

placed the commiphora on this new savanna, and the devastated bush country was colonized by a much more productive vegetation of perennial grasses, together with an abundance of legumes, which were cropped by a variety of game, including the rhino and the elephants themselves, though the conversion of woodland to grassland by elephants and fire could ultimately prove detrimental to the rhinos, whose true habitat is the transitional zone between bush and grassland.

The wholesale destruction of commiphoras was repeated in other areas of the park during droughts in 1968 and 1970–71. In the latter year more than three thousand elephants died because they, like the rhinos, made no attempt to migrate to regions where more forage was available, despite the fact that those in one stricken area, which had missed a local fall of rain, could have obtained food in plenty by migrating only 5 miles up- or downstream, though as soon as rain fell in an adjacent district during the wet season that followed, all the survivors moved out of the drought area within a week, presumably being able to smell rain at a great distance. Daphne Sheldrick concluded from this extraordinary and untypical behavior that the elephants' dry-season range represented their home territory, and that their remaining in this range, even when starving, was an example of a natural law that prevented large herds of roving elephants from cleaning up all available food supplies in one district after another during drought conditions, and devastating the country over a large area.

However, it is impossible even to guess, on the existing data, at the reasons for the repeated destruction of commiphora trees. No doubt elephants have undertaken similar clearances of commiphoras in the past, which have gone unrecorded. There is much that we shall never be able to understand about elephant behavior and society, such as that of the elephants who dragged a dead rhino for some distance and then completely covered it with branches and bushes; or that of the two elephants who supported and guided a blind buffalo for two days; or that of the group of elephants who shoveled earth through a narrow opening in a storehouse in an attempt to cover the severed feet of three hundred of their fellows, shot for laboratory examination during the Tsavo drought; of the many instances of elephants removing the tusks and major bones from slaughtered members of the herd and carrying them away or smashing them against trees or rocks. In one instance three bulls remained by the body of another bull for several days, before finally drawing out his tusks and depositing them at a little distance. In another instance the shoulder blade of a bull that had been shot and the carcass moved to another place was carried back to the precise place of death. Cullen describes how, after it had been found necessary to shoot an elephant with a badly damaged foreleg, "Immediately afterwards, the body was approached by two other elephants. Both circled the body very slowly, after examing it in great detail with the extended tips of their trunks, which were never allowed to make actual contact. Once they made a systematic but unsuccessful attempt to draw the tusks."

These are not idle jungle tales, but recent observations by precise, unsentimental zoologists and park wardens and rangers.

13: Seasonal Migrations of the Herds

The seasonal movements of the grazing herds on the savannas are governed by the irregular cycle of rains and droughts, though in East Africa there is normally a short wet period in November and December and a long one from March to May. On those savannas that are flooded annually, the waters recede early in the dry season, gradually exposing a variety of grasses that attract a succession of herbivores. Elephant and hippo move in to feed on the partially submerged grasses, and their heavy trampling produces a mulch that stimulates a new growth of young shoots for the buffalo. But the plains soon dry out except for a few alkaline pools, and for six months or more become desert-like.

As a result of this seasonal drying up of grazings and water holes, the majority of the savanna game are migratory, traveling 1000 miles or considerably more a year in search of fresh pastures, and many concentrate in the vicinity of lakes and rivers,

increasing the resident population tenfold. During the rainy season on the Serengeti, for example, the blue wildebeest or gnu
are dispersed widely over the plains, grazing the flush of short
grasses, but when these wither early in the summer, they concentrate on the few remaining green areas, and Fuente has described how late in May or early in June small self-contained
groups of wildebeest "gather together in one part of the high
plateau, forming a single immense herd of adult males, females
and calves . . . who set up the characteristic *gnuu gnuu* by
bellowing. . . . The sound echoes endlessly from thousands of
throats . . . interspersed with the shriller whinnying of small
groups of zebra mingling with the solid brown mass of great
antelopes."

Wildebeest are rarely silent, bleating, grunting like giant bull-
frogs, lowing, snorting, and frisking and whisking their tufted
tails so violently while prancing around that they can be heard a
long way off.

Soon the herd is on the move, beginning its 150-mile trek to
the wooded grasslands 1000 feet above the plains, where the
grass is 3 feet high and where there is permanent water and
shade from the summer sun. The zebra, with similar food preferences, migrate with them, and are followed by the majority of
the Tommies, though many of these trek no farther than the
edge of the plains. The Grant's gazelles which, like camels, can
tolerate a rise of several degrees in their body temperature before they begin to lose fluids by sweating, can remain on the
shadeless plains during the hottest weather, ranging over extensive areas of waterless country for forage, which includes the
bitter yellow-green fruits of the 12-inch-high Sodom apple, and
obtaining sufficient liquid from the early morning dew and from
the dry shrubs, because these absorb moisture at night when the
temperature falls and the relative humidity rises.

There is nothing chaotic about this exodus from the plains. "Who, or what, had started it?" asks Evelyn Ames. "What authority brought about all at once that patient submission, leading every small isolated herd to join the whole and keep driving towards new pastures?"

Now that the springbok on the veld and the caribou on the Arctic tundras have been reduced to remnants of their former millions, the migrations of the wildebeest, particularly on their return to the savannas with the first rains, are probably the most spectacular of their kind on earth today, and Audrey Moore has described in *Serengeti* how on one occasion she drove for 30 miles through concentrated herds of game so tightly packed that for half that distance the wildebeest and zebra were unable to move away from the truck. According to George Schaller—to whose *Serengeti: A Kingdom of Predators* I am indebted for many descriptions in this chapter and the next—wildebeest on migration typically travel in regular undulating columns, heads lowered against the stiflingly hot wind, with the sun gleaming through their streaming, fringed white beards, as they "curve their way towards the horizon in long dark disciplined files continuously replenished from a reservoir of huge herds trickling into it from as many plains as are in view. Thick clouds of dust swirl up, and the air is heavy with an odour of earth and manure and the scent of trampled grass."

Their passage is marked by the innumerable deep, winding trenches beaten into furrows by their hooves, and scented by the hot-tar-smelling substance secreted by their front hooves. They lope along with a curiously hunched, oddly wooden gait, sometimes stretching out into a run. The air reverberates with their grunting and the muffled drumming of their hooves. Their plodding tens of thousands—a frieze of animals like a procession in a cave painting—pour over the ridges and funnel down into

Blue wildebeest

the valleys. Under every tree, for mile after mile, groups of wildebeest and zebra crowd together to the limit of the shade, while those unable to find shelter wander about aimlessly in the blazing sun. "If a river bars their way," writes Schaller, "they plunge in, those that hesitate being swept on by the mindless horde behind, until the water is crowded with bellowing animals threshing to get up the slippery banks."

During their absence in the cool woodlands, the tall grasses on the plains seed and wither to the gold of summer corn; dry stubble crackles underfoot; and dust devils, 200 or 300 feet high, twirl over the rises, whirling up into inverted cones or columns that spin, gyrating, across the surface of the earth—as Evelyn Ames has described them. "Fires sweep across the Park," writes Schaller again, "removing undergrowth, killing saplings, scorching tortoises. . . . Flames assault thickets, reducing them in size, then devour dead trees, leaving them as ashy skeletons on the ground. Soon the land is black and bare. . . . Little is left for grazers to eat. . . . Few animals stay behind: a forlorn jackal nosing under a desiccated wildebeest dropping in search of a dung beetle, ungainly ostriches swaying gently along until swallowed by the haze, an occasional Grant's gazelle."

But the fires sweeping over the dry savannas have fertilized the soil for a new growth of grasses, which are further stimulated by the early rains in November and December that refill the lakes. However, these short rains are erratic and fail in some years, compelling the herds to remain in the woodlands or to migrate to and fro unpredictably between woodlands and plains. Schaller has described how "flat-bottomed clouds drifting before the wind . . . herald the onset of the rains. Then towering thunderheads balanced on black pillars of rain bring the fresh showers," which fall typically in sudden heavy downpours in the late afternoon or just before dark. New blades of grass push through the crusted soil and soon the landscape radiates a brilliant green. "Delicate white lilies push up through the hard bare earth," writes Jane Burton, "and the lovely deep pink blossoms of the desert rose open. Aloes send up tall spikes of orange trumpets, providing an abundance of nectar for sunbirds and bees. Small succulent carallumas . . . put out surprisingly large, star-like waxy blossoms, and giant euphorbias are covered with tiny sulphur-yellow flowers."

Everywhere there is great excitement. I quote Schaller again:

Birds begin to court feverishly. A pair of crowned cranes dance with graceful leaps, a male bishop bird flies upward from his reedy perch like a ruby tossed into the wind. Kori bustards patrol the high ground on the plains, flashing their white inflated throat sac and undertail coverts like heliographs from hilltop to hilltop, proclaiming their territory. At this season too European storks, winter visitors from Russia and Poland, wheel in flocks, mere black specks, high in the sky until, in turning, their bodies gleam white in the sunshine.

Wildebeest take off in ecstatic rain dances, leaping and cavorting, bucking like broncos. Zebra, which normally associate in loosely integrated family groups composed of a stallion and his harem of half a dozen or a dozen mares and foals, and in bachelor groups, collect into large herds, with the stallions braying excitedly in wild bursts like hysterical donkeys, before galloping off with the wildebeest toward a storm that may be 5 miles or more distant. They may indeed travel 25 miles in the course of a night to a locality where rain has fallen.

Although the first rains over the savannas coincide with the maximum growth of the grasses in the woodlands, wildebeest and Tommies nevertheless desert this good grazing and return to the plains, where their calves can be born as the grass flushes; and though zebra foal at all seasons of the year, the majority of their young are also born at this time. This return migration is initiated by the Tommies, and they are followed by the zebra in their customary family groups, though they gather in herds when they halt to feed or rest, with the stallions on guard and uttering an occasional yelping bark of warning while their harems are sleeping. Even if a stallion is killed, the group remains intact, for its leadership is taken over by one of the younger stallions, which usually leave their families when from one to four years old and form bachelor herds of a dozen or more, just as young mares are usually enticed away by these bachelors when only fourteen months old to form the nucleus of a new group.

It is during the early stages of this return migration that the wildebeest rut. Since the cows are prolific calvers, this curious rutting time is evidently favorable despite the fact that the bulls can only round up harems during the periodical halts, for as soon as the trek is resumed all form up in large herds again. Moreover, if the rains are late, the calves may be born before the herds reach their grazings, with the result that more than three-quarters of them die from lack of their mother's milk or from attacks by predators. In a normal season, however, the herds split up as soon as they arrive on the plains, and the pregnant cows make for traditional calving grounds where the grass is shortest and offers minimum cover to such predators as lions and hyenas. As Norman Myers has pointed out in *The Long African Day:* "During the last month of pregnancy the female must have enough grass to allow the foetus to increase by several pounds. With a total of sixty extra pounds to carry, she cannot flee so easily from a predator."

Between December and February, and particularly during the last week in January and the first week in February, what has been described as the simultaneous birth of thousands of wildebeest calves takes place. This phenomenon has been held to be a protective measure, inasmuch as the carnivores become sated with the superabundance of food and eventually ignore a large proportion of the calves; but it is possible that this may be a misrepresentation of the facts, and what actually happens is that all the earliest-born calves are taken by hyenas, with the result that two or three weeks later, when more calves are being born than the hyenas can deal with, all appear to have been born at the same time.

However, the wildebeest do have certain protective aids at

this critical time, though these do not prevent heavy losses among the calves when the herds are stampeded by predators. Thus, although most of the calves are dropped at dawn, the cows are reputed to be able, if threatened by a predator, to interrupt or delay the expulsion of the fetus, providing that the head is not extruded. Moreover, the calves can struggle to their feet within three to ten minutes after birth, though to encourage them to keep moving and thus strengthen their legs, most cows apparently prevent their calves suckling for the first few minutes by moving their hindquarters away from them. As an additional strengthening measure, other members of the herd may even continually butt a newborn calf, forcing it to run away from them or to struggle to its feet repeatedly when knocked down.

Birth is an extremely rapid process with all antelopes, and many young are on their feet within two minutes (though some, it is true, not for forty or fifty minutes); and Rennie Bere has described how on one occasion when he was watching a herd of topi galloping across the grassland, a doe stopped and dropped her fawn. While she licked it clean and nuzzled it, her companions waited until it got to its feet and was able to run with them within fifteen minutes. Shortly afterward more does also dropped their fawns, with the other members of the herd providing a protective screen against possible predators. On the other hand, many young antelope freeze in their "forms" when danger threatens, even though fully capable of fleeing with the herd, and the does of some species that collect in small groups with their newborn young remain in one place for the first three or four days, and do not rejoin the herd until the fawns have been weaned after three or four months' lactation.

From October to June the grazing pressure on the savannas by the tens of thousands of herbivores is intense, and the ultimate controlling regulator of their numbers is the amount of food available, which is profoundly influenced by the distribution of rainfall. As Schaller has pointed out, "Without rigid controls hoofed animals tend to increase up to and beyond the capacity of the range to support them." By keeping the grazing herds on the move, predators, especially the hunting dogs, force the game to disperse to fresh pastures, thereby increasing the stocking capacity of a range, while the mixing of the herds when they are hunted ensures the continual introduction of fresh strains, just as the toll taken of mature males creates vacancies for younger males to introduce new blood.

The predators' effect on the actual numbers of prey is strictly limited. Schaller has estimated that the Serengeti population of perhaps 2000 lions must kill between 40,000 and 72,000 individual prey annually. The 3000 hyenas would account for a further 25,000 to 30,000 adult prey, and other predators bring the total yearly kill to between 75,000 and over 110,000; but, with the major predators preying on more than twenty different species, this toll represents only 5 percent of the prey available. Thus, although hyenas kill up to 19,000 wildebeest calves every year on the Serengeti plains, more than twice this number die from lack of their mother's milk, starvation, or disease, and hyenas and lions together in fact take a toll of only about 50 percent of the natural increase in the wildebeest population which, as we have seen, has more than doubled in the past decade. This apparent heavy toll by predators has not therefore exercised any significant control over their numbers. On the contrary, the wildebeest themselves appear to have been maintaining a form of birth control, for whereas, according to Schaller, "In the early 1960's, when the population was fairly small, about a third of the cows had a calf in their second year, by the late 1960's, with the population high, only about 5 per cent had a calf in their second year." Thus it is reasonable to assume that if lions and hyenas had increased their toll, the wildebeest would have countered by raising their birthrate, just as lions apparently automatically adjust their own numbers to those of their prey by producing larger or smaller litters. Nevertheless, despite this birth control and heavy predation, the wildebeest population has continued to increase dramatically on the Serengeti.

Similarly, the Tommies are able to maintain their enormous populations by producing, when necessary, two sets of fawns in one year as a counter to the fearful toll of pregnant does, and also of mature bucks reluctant to leave their harem territories on the instant, exacted by hunting dogs and cheetahs, and also by lions and leopards when the herds are grazing among trees or in bush; and the equally heavy slaughter of fawns by hyenas, jackals, servals, caracals, baboons, and the larger birds of prey. But a point must be reached when overgrazing or stress from overcrowding or a prolonged drought will result in starvation and/or disease, and a population crash. As has been stressed in previous chapters the only significant effect that predation can have on a successful species of prey is to retard population explosions.

14: Everyday Life Among Cheetahs and Lions

Although the main predator of the African plains in terms of total weight of prey killed is the lion, the natural hunter of the swift antelope and gazelles, both in Africa and India, is obviously the cheetah, with its long legs and nonretractable claws serving the same purpose as an athlete's spikes, powerful muscles, and supple spine. Cheetahs employ two basic hunting techniques. One involves stalking up to a grazing herd, crouching and freezing whenever an individual raises its head, until within 30 yards of the selected animal, then waiting until the latter has turned away, before launching itself at it. Alternatively, the cheetah walks slowly and openly across the plain toward a herd, which does not panic though watching the cheetah closely. When the latter is within about 80 yards, the does begin to move off, but bucks holding territories may delay until the cheetah is within 50 yards. The cheetah then singles out one buck, perhaps a little isolated from the others, and bounds toward it with an electrifying acceleration, reaching 45 miles per hour from its standing start in approximately two seconds, and possibly 70 miles per hour at top speed, when its body arches almost into a circle, with its hind feet striking the ground in front of its head. However, although a cheetah is reported to have clocked 71.65 miles per hour on a racecourse, some observers consider its maximum speed to lie within the 55- to 65-mile-per-hour limit. The relevant point is that no African gazelle or antelope is capable of speeds much in excess of 50 miles per hour. Nevertheless, if a successful kill is to be made, the cheetah must normally launch its attack from a distance of not more than 200 yards, and if it is not able to seize its prey by the throat, or bowl it over with a sweep of a forepaw, after a run of 500 yards at most, it abandons the chase since the energy expended in this explosive burst is so great that at its conclusion it is panting at the rate of 150 breaths a minute.

Although African cheetahs are known to hunt twenty-five different kinds of prey, including hares and birds and infrequently such large antelope as wildebeest, they rely mainly on impalas and the Tommies and Grant's gazelles; and most of the cheetahs on the Serengeti—perhaps 200 or 250 in number—are reported to migrate with the gazelles when they trek off the plains in the dry season. Nevertheless, although they are almost invariably successful in catching the fawns, about half the adult gazelles escape their attacks. They seem to be more successful with impala, for in the Kruger National Park, forty-seven kills resulted from sixty-five pursuits, despite the exceptional agility of impalas that enables them to cover 70 feet in three bounds or to clear a road 35 feet wide with a single 10-foot high leap. When baboons are foraging on the open grasslands in groups of thirty to fifty, with the vulnerable mothers, infants, and juveniles protected ahead, behind, and on either side by the powerful males, armed with large canines, impalas often feed with them for protection against attacks by cheetahs.

In some areas cheetahs associate in small groups; in others, such as the Serengeti, they usually hunt alone, particularly if they are adult males, while females with cubs usually avoid other cheetahs. Joy Adamson noted that while mother and cubs were always overjoyed to meet up again, after the latter had begun to hunt duiker on their own at ages varying from fourteen to twenty months, none of the cubs subsequently intruded on their mother's hunting territory, or on each other's in the 63 square miles of Kenya's Northern Frontier District to which the mother had gradually introduced them before they left her when she mated again. Cheetahs are such specialist hunters that they may always have had difficulty in maintaining their populations—they are already extinct in India, where their main prey, the blackbuck, has been almost exterminated.

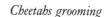

Cheetahs grooming

Moreover, despite the fact that the family group tears its kills apart as quickly as possible, 10 percent of these are probably lost to lions and hyenas, while even a menacing phalanx of vultures, gradually closing in on foot, can frighten them off. Furthermore, although the female is constantly moving her litter of from two to five cubs from one hiding place to another, and may do so more than twenty times in six weeks, carrying them by their napes until they are three weeks old, about 50 percent of them are taken by lions and leopards and particularly by hyenas before they are six months old, though to the human eye their curious gray capes of silky hair render them almost invisible when they are lying in patches of long grass.

It is perhaps significant that in the Nairobi National Park, where hyenas are scarce, the density of cheetahs averages 1 to 2 square miles, whereas on the Serengeti, where hyenas are numerous, there may be only one to 20 or even 50 square miles. Cheetahs hunt mainly in the early morning and evening, resting for most of the remainder of the day on termite mounds or in low trees, watching the antelope herds. Although they are excellent tree climbers, they are not physically adapted to climbing and, according to Joy Adamson, frequently injure their long, fragile legs when leaping down from heights of 20 feet or higher, particularly when between four and eight months old.

The preferred habitats of lions are the open grass plains and lightly wooded savanna, where high grass, belts of acacia, bush bordering watercourses, dry river-ravines, rocks and kopjes provide covert, but they also inhabit dense bush and explore forested mountainsides to heights above 11,000 feet, though rarely entering the rain forest. Unlike tigers, they are tolerant of the sun, often lying all day in the open, even when shade is close by, and inhabit desert scrub and roam across semidesert.

The type of prey killed by lions depends upon the nature of their habitat, the relative abundance of particular prey and especially the ease with which these can be obtained. Hunting groups are smaller when gazelles are the prey, larger in the case of the more meaty wildebeest. As Norman Carr has stated:

> What the optimum predator-prey should be, in a given area, is difficult . . . to assess, but it depends to a large extent on the vulnerability of the prey animal rather than on the actual total number of them. For example, a large quantity of animals who live permanently on a plain would not support such a large lion population as a lesser number of animals who frequented bush-covered country, because a lion needs cover in order to stalk its prey and would take a far greater toll from the bush country than from the plains.

Colonel J. Stevenson-Hamilton approached this problem from a different angle, pointing out that when game is relatively more numerous when pasturage is good it is more widely distributed and therefore more difficult to locate by large predators such as lions, but when forage is scarce and game less numerous then it is more easily located and killed because it is more concentrated in the limited number of grazing grounds and also at drinking places. Therefore, in these latter conditions, and particularly if there is a succession of dry seasons and poor pasturage, lions paradoxically increase in numbers. But if a period of good grazing seasons follows, the game (initially fewer) scatters over the ample pasturage, while the lions (initially more numerous) are unable to kill sufficient prey to feed large prides, with the result that the juveniles starve or are killed by the adult members of the prides when attempting to seize their share of the meat, and the lionesses are unable to produce as many litters or rear as many cubs.

Whatever the conditions, four out of five hunts are likely to be unsuccessful because, after the patient stalk and charge at 30 or 35 miles per hour, the prey may prove too swift or agile. Wildebeest, hartebeest, Tommies, and Grant's gazelles are all capable of 50 miles per hour, zebra of 45 miles per hour, giraffes of 37 miles per hour, and buffalo of 35 miles per hour. Even a charge from a distance of only 30 yards may be unsuccessful, and a lion lacks stamina for a long pursuit. Schaller concluded that lion hunts are most often successful when conducted at night or from covert of riverine thickets, when upwind, when more than one lioness is taking part, or when the hunt is directed at a solitary animal rather than at a herd. More often than not, a hunting pride does in fact select an individual that can be isolated from the herd, though switching its attention to the herd if the victim eludes it. There seems to be no doubt that lions also employ comparatively sophisticated hunting techniques involving tactical cooperation, with one individual or group driving the game toward other members of the pride concealed in ambush.

Medium-sized antelope such as the wildebeest, particularly the bulls, are the main prey, and constitute 50 percent of the lion kills on most East African savannas, though only 25 percent on the Serengeti from which the wildebeest are absent for half a year. In Zambia, however, 75 percent of the kills are buffalo, but this is exceptional, for although more than six thousand of the fifty thousand adult and young buffalo on the Serengeti die every year, only one-third of these fall to lions. Crocodiles seize some calves when they are wallowing in the shallows, and the remainder succumb to starvation or disease.

Nor does lion predation prevent the buffalo population from increasing, for many of the victims are surplus bulls—either stragglers from the bachelor groups of a score or so that tend to lag behind the main herd, composed of several hundred cows and young beasts, accompanied perhaps by forty or fifty bulls that accept the regime of one, or two, dominant bulls, or more particularly aged bulls which have been expelled from, or have voluntarily left, the herd during the rut in July and August, to roam alone or in small groups along wooded river courses, where these massive beasts, up to 3000 pounds in weight, are more easily tackled by lions, though the latter are frequently killed when attempting to bring down the younger, more active bulls. Although many of the old loners that survive return to the security of the herds after the rut, those over twelve years old continue to live a solitary existence.

Warthogs, which feed by day when lions are usually dozing, and den up in abandoned aardvark labyrinths at night when lions are hunting, are surprisingly high up on the roll of lion prey. But, in fact, although lions normally hunt by night on savannas where there is little stalking cover, they may hunt by day in the dry season when the game concentrates along bush-covered or wooded riverbanks; while during the rainy season, when tall vegetation renders stalking easier, warthogs are vulnerable. When the ground has been softened by rain, lions often dig them out of their cavernous dens, and Schaller watched one lioness digging for an hour until, when she had exposed 2½ yards of the burrow, she was able to grab a sow and pull it out after tugging for eight minutes. Warthogs are also preyed on by leopards, while jackals kill the piglets, with the result that only about a quarter of these survive their first year. However, this high rate of mortality is offset by the fact that the surviving females are generally mature when only eighteen months old and are extremely prolific.

The size of a pride's hunting territory is also dependent on the nature of their environment and the relevant abundance of prey, and the fact that every pride holds a territory spreads the lion

population fairly evenly over the habitats of their prey, while
the dispersal of the members of a pride over their territory enables them to locate prey more efficiently. The size of the territory may also vary seasonally, as on the Serengeti where, according to Schaller, it ranges from 15 square miles during the
rainy season when the numbers of game are at their peak to 150
square miles during the dry season when almost all the game has
left the plains. It also depends on the numerical strength of the
pride, for this and also its composition vary from day to day, as
its members disperse singly or in small groups. Indeed all the
known members of a pride may never be seen together at one
time over a period of years. The various territories overlap extensively, and that of a breakaway splinter group may even lie
wholly within one of their relatives. However, neighboring
prides seldom meet, and nomadic groups of young lions, which
may range over upward of 1800 square miles, usually avoid contact with resident prides. The chances of confrontation between
the two are reduced because the latter do not hunt over all parts
of their territory equally, but spend much of the year in that
part most plentifully supplied with prey and water. According
to Schaller, "a pride may not even be aware of intrusions into
the peripheral parts of its territory and nomads sometimes reside
there for weeks as squatters."

Carr has described how when a lioness comes into season she
leaves the pride and goes off with the dominant lion, followed
perhaps by one or more male rivals:

> This honeymoon will continue for two weeks or so and is
> quite liable to cause a split in the family disposition if any of
> the rivals who tag on decide to have a trial of strength for pos-
> session of a bride. If the patriarch is able to maintain his su-
> premacy they will all go back to the pride and no drastic
> change results. If, on the other hand, the leader is ousted by

one of his rivals, either on his honeymoon or on his return to the family, he will probably go off on his own and might in the course of time pick up a male companion in the same predicament as himself.

Two such companions have been described by Evelyn Ames:

In the grass beside the track lay a fine male lion. For a few seconds, he looked directly at us, chin lifted, amber eyes half closed, then his attention abruptly shifted and focussed on another big male stalking towards him through the trees. When only ten feet or so of sparkling grass divided them, the nearer lion stood up, advanced and the two greeted one another—rubbed their huge shaggy heads affectionately against one another, over and over, uttering little moaning grunts of endearment like those we had heard between the mothers and cubs of our big pride. With a last placing together of their wide foreheads, they separated and looked about consideringly, then walked off, side by side, into the rising sun.

A rejected male may team up with a nomadic lioness who will hunt for him, but less than 10 percent of male lions survive into old age, because once they have been evicted from their prides by younger lions or by nomads, they cannot share in the prides' kills and are not accepted by the nomadic groups, though these, having no settled territories to defend, usually accept strangers of their own age group. Almost all the young males leave the prides into which they were born by the time they are three and a half years old—though occasionally one may remain to dominate the pride with his father—and a few lionesses also become nomads when between two and a half and three and a half years old. The young males, many or most of whom are blood brothers or of the same age group, may continue to associate for months or years, though from time to time they leave the group to mate with nomadic lionesses, in whose company they spend a few days or weeks before returning to their fellows. This constant emigration of the younger members, together with the death from time to time of an adult, stabilizes the size of the prides.

The detailed studies of the large prides of lions on the plains of the Serengeti, with its seasonal comings and goings of game, have tended to overemphasize the prevalence of large prides. In harsh environments, such as the semidesert of the Northern Frontier District, lions tend to associate in pairs rather than prides, with territories varying in size from 40 to 100 square miles, depending upon the numbers of game, though when cubs are born the lion leaves his mate. Large prides—one of thirty-seven has been recorded—are characteristic of an open plain environment, and typically consist of from one to four adult lions with fifteen lionesses, juveniles, and cubs. The majority of the lionesses, who are usually related, remain together for the duration of their lives, honeymoon periods excepted. Although it is they who are responsible for upward of 90 percent of a pride's kills, the male or males play an important role in defending the hunting territory and in protecting their mates and cubs. If one of two adult males in a breeding pride is killed, the survivor may not be able to withstand the attacks of a nomadic group, which takes over the lionesses and kills the cubs; while a pride that includes no adult lion may experience the same fate. On the other hand, two or three lionesses may establish a matriarchal society, and an association between two lionesses may last for several years, with one suckling both litters of cubs if her companion is injured; though from time to time such female groups may be joined by males from an adjoining territory, or themselves overlap another pride's territory.

A secure male-held territory ensures that the pride's lionesses have secluded strongholds in thickets and kopjes in which to

Lions—male, female, and cubs

rear their cubs. In a pride deprived of one of its males, less than
8 percent of the cubs may survive, whereas a pride protected by
three males may rear 60 percent. The social cohesion of a male-
dominated pride also gives a sense of security to its members,
and according to Schaller, lionesses cannot raise adequate
numbers of cubs without this security. Thus resident prides
tend to be sedentary and remain in their territories, even when
their adult members are hungry and the cubs starving because,
as on the Serengeti, the game has emigrated; but nomadic lionesses, emigrating with the game, and therefore well-fed, lack the

security of the pride and are seldom able to rear cubs even if
they give birth to them. Moreover, lionesses often fail to come
into season, but when one member of a pride does so, this apparently stimulates her companions, and birth peaks tend to coincide with this phenomenon and also, on the Serengeti, with
the return of the migrant game. This irregular breeding of the
lionesses, together with the very high mortality rate among the
cubs—less than half of which survive to maturity—is the main
regulator of the lion population. One lioness, for example, succeeded in rearing only six cubs out of seven litters over a period
of twelve years, while of seventy-nine cubs born to the lionesses
of two prides, fifty-three were lost, eleven being killed by other
lions, one by a leopard, and one by a hyena, while fifteen
starved and twenty-five died from unknown causes.

The three of four cubs in a litter remain hidden away for
varying periods after birth. Some are visited by other members
of the pride before they can walk, but the majority do not meet
the pride until they can accompany their mothers at the age of
five or six weeks, and are not regular members until eight or ten
weeks old, when they can keep up with the pride on its travels.
These first few weeks are critical, because the cubs in their lairs
are easy prey for hyenas and other predators when their mothers
are away hunting, whereas, once they are strong enough, litters
of varying ages may amalgamate and can be guarded by any
lioness and suckle indiscriminately from any with milk. A single
"nursery" may include as many as six lionesses and seventeen
juveniles.

Joy Adamson's experiences with Elsa and other lionesses in
northern Kenya indicate that they are extremely attached to
their cubs, bringing food to them for many months after their
first eight weeks on milk, and teaching them to hunt. The cubs
cannot kill efficiently until they are at least eighteen months old,

and at that age, or earlier, experience their second critical period when their mothers mate again and drive them away, and other members of the pride rob them of their share of kills; but paradoxically on the plains where, it is asserted, large prides are advantageous to the species, the adults, both male and female, may display virtually no concern for the cubs' welfare. Thus, during the dry season on the Serengeti as high a proportion as 90 percent of the cubs may die, not because of the seasonal scarcity of prey, but because they are unable to obtain their share of what may be the only prey available—the small gazelles, for while the adult males do not necessarily feed first, as often stated, all the members of the pride crowd around a kill with savagely snapping jaws and flashing claws in an ill-tempered melee that results in minor injuries to themselves and no opportunity for the cubs to sneak in for scraps. It must be said that, under these conditions, the female of the species is more ruthless than the male, for whereas the lion often allows the cubs, but not their mothers, to share the meat of a large kill, the latter not only bolt any meat themselves rather than share it with the cubs, but frequently actually snatch meat from them.

Schaller has postulated that, rather than return with meat to her own small cubs hidden away at a distance, a lioness, "as an intensely social creature, prefers to be with other pride members than separated from them with her small cubs;" but one finds it difficult to believe that this can be the case except under conditions of extreme hunger, though it could be argued that the free-for-all at the kill ensures the survival of the adult lions (the defenders of the hunting territory) and the adult females (the food providers), and that the majority of the cubs are expendable, since the survival of only a small proportion of these is sufficient to maintain the lion population. It would seem much more probable that such behavior results from a pride being too large to kill sufficient game to feed all its members during the season of scarcity.

The fact that the cubs of these large Serengeti prides may be literally starving in no way influences the pride's daily routine. They still pass twenty or twenty-one hours of every day sleeping or dozing or just sitting, and cover an average of only 3 miles a day in hunting. Lions can only be described as lazy by nature, for the habits of man-eating lions, which may travel more than 30 miles in a night, are unnatural. One comparatively energetic, 4½-year-old lion (accompanied by a middle-aged lioness) averaged, for example, 7½ miles a day during a nine-day period of observation, but although he ate on seven nights, not once did he kill for himself, feeding three times on hyena kills and four times on the kills of other lionesses; while a nomadic lion, which averaged 6 miles a day over a three-week period, seldom bothered to hunt, ate only seven times, and bestirred himself only every few days to trek several miles to drink at a pool. In short, lions usually hunt only when finally impelled by hunger—a wounded lion can survive for seventeen days without food— when each member of the pride may gorge on up to 75 pounds of meat or one-fifth of its own weight if a male.

15: Hyena Clans

Because of the scarcity of game for half the year, lions on the Serengeti unexpectedly obtain much of their food by scavenging from hyenas, while in the Ngorongoro Crater, hyena kills, mainly of wildebeest, zebra, and Tommies, provide them with a major source of food; though unless they arrive at a carcass within a few minutes of the kill, only scraps are likely to remain. According to Trevor Simon, writing in *Animals*, "There are a number of lions who wait patiently on high ground and scan the floor of the crater for any . . . signs that the hyenas are at work. With their excellent sight and acute hearing they can detect a kill at a range of over two miles."

The most extensive unflooded caldera in the world, the steep, brush-covered bastion walls, 12 miles from rim to rim, of the Ngorongoro's 100 square miles of rolling grasslands, willow-green lake, forests and hills, rise 2000 feet abruptly over the Serengeti plains. There are some 1500 carnivores, including 70

199

lions, between 420 and 450 hyenas, and 500 jackals, in the Ngorongoro and more than 20,000 ungulates, mainly wildebeest, zebra, and gazelles, with the Grant's grazing the tall grass on the sides of the crater and the Tommies concentrating on the alkaline pastures near the lake, where they can drink. Because rainwater oozes perpetually from the crater walls and because the swamps never dry out, more than three-quarters of the game are permanently resident.

Of the three species of hyena—spotted, brown, and striped—the spotted outnumber all the other carnivores combined in some areas of East Africa; but it has only recently been rediscovered that hyenas are not exclusively scavengers, as they were generally believed to be except by the old hunters, but predators in their own right, besides catching termites when they swarm on their nuptial flights, and fishing in shallow waters. They are not, as usually stated, averse to water, not only spending hours lying in pools, but also diving into 5 feet of water to drag out a carcass or following a hunted wildebeest into a lake.

The spotted hyenas in the Ngorongoro indeed kill more than 75 percent of their own prey. By day they follow the traditional role of scavengers, working mainly in ones and twos, and driving cheetahs and even lionesses from kills, though not daring to threaten an adult male lion, evading his irate charges and sneaking hopefully around his kill for as long as thirty-five hours. However, two young male lions and a mob of giggling and growling hyenas may feed together on a wildebeest, and Simon took a remarkable photograph of six young lions and seven or eight hyenas eating at the same kill at night.

It is at night that the spotted hyenas become predators. It is suggested that game cannot see as well as the hyenas in the dark, with the result that their speed is reduced to 20 or 25 miles per hour, or 12 to 15 miles per hour in the case of zebra, whereas

hyenas can run at 35 and possibly 40 miles per hour and bring
down a wildebeest after a pursuit of 3 miles or less. Moreover,
having much larger hearts than any of the cats, they can keep up
a fairly fast lope for 10 miles or more. Hyenas are generally reported to pack only when following lions or when gathering at a
carcass, but when hunting zebra, they do so in packs of from ten
to thirty or forty, and Hugo and Jane van Lawick-Goodall have
described in *Innocent Killers* a pack of about thirty hunting zebra
in the Ngorongoro:

> The scattered groups of zebras had massed together into a
> huge striped band, well over two hundred strong. As this had
> cantered along we could see several stallions defending the
> rear, pausing every so often to bite back at the leading hyenas,
> their ears pressed close to their necks. The air was constantly
> vibrating to the shrill braying barks of the hunted zebras, and
> their hoofs thundered across the moonlit hillside . . . I saw
> one of [the hyenas] suddenly fly up into the air, about a foot
> higher than the zebras' backs, and I presumed it had been
> kicked. It rolled over twice when it landed, but got up and
> went on running. For about fifteen minutes we followed the
> hunt and then, in ones and twos and small groups, the hyenas
> dropped back, giving up in the face of that solid wall of zebras
> and the active defence of the stallions.

In a favorable environment hyenas form clans, and it is possible that the various clans have preferences for particular types of
prey. Of those watched by the Van Lawick-Goodalls in the
Ngorongoro, for example, one clan frequently but untypically
hunted zebra, while another concentrated on wildebeest, especially their newborn calves, and Myers has suggested that these
hyenas may have become particularly active as predators after
the lion population had been reduced by the 1962 plague of
flies, and when so many wildebeest and zebra had been too
weakened to escape their attacks. Clans with more than a

hundred members have been recorded, and their society is matriarchal, with the females, weighing 130 pounds, usually larger than the males. Dens with cubs are the focal points around which a clan's social life revolves, and Jane van Lawick-Goodall has described how visiting usually begins at sundown and continues on and off throughout the night:

> Some hyenas just wander past . . . pausing only to greet their friends, but there are many also who visit for long periods . . . lying near the den, playing with the cubs or adults already there, greeting newcomers. Usually a number of cubs, old enough to move around without their mothers, wander across every evening to a den where smaller cubs are living, stay there throughout the night, and return to their own home dens every morning.

Although the cubs are strong enough when four months old to play about in the vicinity of the den, their parents neither bring food regularly to them, nor lead them to kills, with the result that they are suckled for as long as a year or eighteen months, when they are almost full-grown, in contrast to the few weeks' lactation of most carnivores. On the Serengeti the erratic migrations of the game result in famine seasons even among hyenas, compelling those permanently resident on the plains to leave their cubs alone in their dens for three or four days at a time while they travel twenty or thirty miles in search of wildebeest or zebra, though they have often been known to travel fifty miles to and from a kill in a single night. Other clans, however, break up and follow the migratory herds for several months, hunting and associating amicably with members of other clans, since no territorial rights are involved.

In the Ngorongoro, however, where prey is abundant all the year around, the Van Lawick-Goodalls found that the crater's 100 square miles was divided up among eight resident clans,

Spotted hyenas

with each clan patrolling its territory regularly and scent-marking its boundaries with the glands under their tails; but although territories were defended fiercely, they were not permanently stable in size, for they were invaded by other clans equally fiercely. One clan of sixty, known as the "Scratching Rocks," for example, doubled their original 6 square miles during the course of a year at the expense of one or other of three clans with adjacent territories; and Jane van Lawick-Goodall has given a dramatic account of one such battle for territory:

Bloody Mary and Lady Astor, leading matriarchs of the Scratching Rocks clan, began to run fast over the moonlit plain, their tails aggressively curled over their broad rumps. Behind them ran some eighteen other members of the clan.

About sixty yards ahead two hyenas of the neighbouring Lakeside Clan were resting close to the boundary of their territory. It seems that they were fast asleep, for when they got up Bloody Mary and Lady Astor were only a few yards from them. One of the pair was lucky and escaped running for its life, but the other was not quick enough. Bloody Mary and Lady Astor seized hold of it and a few moments later it was practically hidden from sight as more and more of its enemies rushed in to bite and rend at its body. The night was filled with the fearsome roars and low whooping calls and growls of the triumphant Scratching Rocks clan and the horrible screams of their victim.

Suddenly, however, a group of ten hyenas of the Lakeside Clan . . . came racing in tight formation towards the battleground . . . it was within its territory and the hyenas, as they ran to defend their "rights", were confident and aggressive. The unruly mob of Scratching Rocksters retreated hastily. . . . For a short distance the Lakeside Clan pursued them, but once they had crossed the boundary into Scratching Rocks territory they stopped. . . .

Meanwhile the Scratching Rocksters, once they were well within their own territory, also stopped, and the two rival clans faced each other, both keeping tight formation. Each individual held its tail curled stiffly over its rump, and the low growling whooping calls sounded louder and louder. . . . And all the time both clans were swelling in numbers as more and more members, attracted by the calls of battle, hurried to the scene.

Suddenly I saw the shadowy forms of Bloody Mary and Lady Astor rush forward, side by side, and a moment later the rest of the clan was beside its leaders. For a short while the Lakesiders held their ground, and there were loud roars and shrill giggling, chuckling sounds as hyenas briefly attacked and chased each other. . . . And then the Lakeside Clan retreated, running back into its own territory. After chasing for a short distance the Scratching Rocksters, who had once more crossed their boundary . . . stopped. Again the two clans faced each other, the whooping calls filling the air until the Lakesiders, reaching a peak of frenzy, rushed forward to renew hostilities. Another brief skirmish and then the Scratching Rocks Clan once more retreated into its own territory.

And so it went on, each clan surging forward in turn behind its leaders and then suddenly braking and rushing back from the aggressive charge of the other. Eventually there were between thirty and forty hyenas on each side. . . .

Twenty minutes from the start of the affair the skirmishing suddenly ended and members of both clans moved farther and farther into their own territories.

16: Nomadic Wild Dogs

In Africa hyenas maintain an uneasy relationship with wild dogs. At one time hyenas and dogs may be lying in the shade of the same tree, with a hyena sleeping in the middle of a pack and actually touching the dogs on either side, or creeping up to a sleeping dog to lick beneath its tail. At another time a pack of dogs may torment a hyena mercilessly, savaging its hindquarters. Hunting packs of dogs are often accompanied by one or two hyenas, "tagging along behind, risking having their rumps nipped"—in Schaller's words. The dogs inhabit the savannas and open bush from the southern fringes of the Sahara to the Cape, and across the continent from east to west, regularly roaming to an altitude of 15,000 feet on Mount Kenya and occasionally to 19,000 feet on Kilimanjaro. They also hunt in deserts, where they can probably survive for several weeks without water, and in the desert of northern Sudan, Michael Mason found their tracks around dead ostriches and dorcas gazelles, and shot some members of a pack of fourteen.

Prior to the recent studies of the Van Lawick-Goodalls and Hans Kruuk, our knowledge of the habits and social organization of the African hunting dogs was, like that of their forest relatives in India and other parts of Asia, mainly restricted to random notes and a mass of speculation, invariably hostile. We now know that an average pack of dogs numbers nine or ten, though packs of more than forty have been reported. Nineteenth-century South African hunters refer to packs of several hundred, while more recently Karen Blixen (Isak Dinesen), author of *Out of Africa*, has described an unusual encounter with some five hundred dogs at midday in the Masai Reserve in Tanzania:

> They came along in a slow canter, in the strangest way, looking neither right nor left, as if they had been frightened by something, or as if they were travelling fast with a fixed purpose on a track. . . . They were running in a long file, two or three or four side by side; it took some time before the whole procession had passed us. In the middle of it, Farah said: 'These dogs are very tired, they have run a long way.'

Each pack has its own territory, and five packs may be hunting on the fringes of a sixth's without ever crossing over its scent-marked boundaries, but the extent of a territory varies erratically and is not permanent because the dogs are nomadic, remaining in one district for several days or weeks and then being replaced overnight by another pack without any evidence of conflict, and not reappearing again for a period of months perhaps, during which time it may have been identified in places 70 miles apart. But in the majority of instances, the size of a pack's territory and also their nomadism are clearly influenced by the relative abundance or scarcity of game and the latter's migratory movements, and also by the pupping periods of any bitches in the pack.

For example, when the herds of wildebeest and zebra are

congregated on the plains of the Serengeti in February, the hunting territory of a pack, that includes a bitch with young pups, may be only 15 square miles, but when the game emigrate in May the pack may have to range over 75 square miles in search of prey. Indeed, on the Sabi game reserve in South Africa, one pack of sixty to seventy is reported by Stevenson-Hamilton to have hunted over 1500 square miles. It is perhaps because the game has become excessively wary and difficult to kill after persistent hunting that a pack will suddenly abandon such an apparently perfect hunting ground as the grasslands of the Ngorongoro Crater, where the bulk of the herds are permanently resident.

The dogs usually hunt in the cooler hours just before dawn or very early in the morning, and again before dusk or in the moonlight. The hunt is almost invariably activated by one or two members of the pack which, on waking, wander over to the sleeping groups of their fellows, greeting, licking, and playing with them, until all have been roused and are ready to move off. Jane van Lawick-Goodall has described how, just as the sun was setting, the leader of one pack rose to his feet, yawned as he stretched himself, and trotted over to where a bitch and two dogs lay together:

> At his approach they jumped up and all four began nosing and licking each other's lips . . . their squeaks gradually changing to frenzied twittering. In a moment all the adult dogs had joined them and soon the pack was swirling round and round in the greeting ceremony. . . . And then, as suddenly as it began, the wild flurry of activity subsided and the pack started to trot away from the den on its morning hunt.

This particular pack was led by one dog, Ghengis, who, walking some 10 yards ahead of his pack, most of whom followed in single file, both initiated and directed the hunt, determining its line of advance and ultimately selecting a particular quarry. A pack may, however, fan out at some stage in the hunt, maintaining contact with a clear, soft, bell-like *hoo-hoo-hoo*, repeated five or six times with a pause between each cuckoo-like *hoo*.

The dogs may prey on gazelles and young wildebeest, though according to C. A. W. Guggisberg, wildebeest cows with calves are usually able to make their getaway when other members of the herd form up in a protective screen and advance toward the dogs, which then lose interest; but other antelopes and, to a lesser degree, zebra, are also hunted, while a pack of twenty are capable of stampeding a herd of forty or fifty buffalo. Indeed they are known, like hyenas, to have attacked and killed elephant calves, despite the presence of adults, and Cullen cites an extraordinary incident on the shores of Uganda's Lake Edward, where the warden saw a full-grown hippo being set upon early one morning by a pack of wild dogs:

> The dogs—which were silent, were all around the hippo, which was endeavouring to get to the water. Some were actually worrying the big beast by jumping at its chest and legs. When the warden intervened, the dogs desisted from that attack, but then—having left the hippo—they formed a semicircle round two elephants, which were obviously scared and trumpeted loudly through raised trunks, at the same time retreating backwards.

A warden in Tanzania has also recorded a lone bull rhino being teased by eleven wild dogs as it walked slowly along surrounded by the pack; while in another instance a ranger "came across the scene of a very definite encounter between wild dog and rhino, which continued for about two miles. When this large rhino was subsequently shot, it was noticed that the heels of all four feet were quite badly torn, and there was a fair-sized gash on one leg. There was no shortage of small game in this area, so this was not a case of wild dogs attacking a rhino out of desperation."

Normally, where game is abundant, the dogs tend to hunt one particular species in preference to others—impala in open bush, Tommies on the plains and also in the Ngorongoro, where these gazelles, and in particular the bucks, form 60 percent of their kills; and a pack specializing in zebra hunting has been known to trot out 16 miles from its base, passing through herds of thousands of gazelles and other potential prey en route, before ultimately selecting a zebra mare and killing her foal. During the dry season the Ghengis pack did not locate prey until it had traveled 5 miles from its base, and its subsequent pursuit of one of a group of three Grant's gazelles was one of the longest witnessed by the Van Lawick-Goodalls, for it continued for 3½ miles, with the pack running at a steady 30 miles per hour, with spurts of up to 35 miles per hour. Contrary to the prevalent belief that wild dogs kill by running down their victim relentlessly over a long distance, most pursuits in open country are apparently abandoned if the prey is not brought down within a distance of 2½ to 3 miles, and the dogs rest before setting out on another hunt. Indeed, only thirty-nine of the ninety-one hunts observed by the Van Lawick-Goodalls were successful, though under more favorable conditions the success rate may be as high as 85 to 90 percent, while during the wildebeests' calving season, a pack may kill twice as much prey as it requires, with each dog averaging 12 pounds of meat a day; but the surplus is not wasted, for it supplies hyenas and jackals and thereby preserves the lives of other animals.

Stevenson-Hamilton has described, in *Wild Life in South Africa*, how in bush country a hunting pack of dogs, with heads and tails held low, ramble along silently at hounds' pace:

On coming on a fresh "line" there is no increase of pace, but the leaders prick their great round ears, and jump at intervals straight up and down to get a view over the top of the grass and low scrub. Now some impala can be seen down an aisle of the bush calmly browsing, and immediately the whole pack spreads out noiselessly to encircle it. A ewe raising her head quickly in an interval of feeding, catches sight of one of the sinister forms . . . she snorts loudly and in a moment, as by one impulse, the pack dashes in. Away in all directions . . . rush the antelope, springing high into the air, and in the confusion often impeding one another. . . . One or two are instantly . . . pulled down, and the rest of the pursuers, splitting up into smaller detachments, relentlessly pursue the . . . individuals which they have singled out.

On the plains the dogs make no attempt either to stalk or to approach under cover to a herd, but walk slowly and openly up to it, crouching slightly. Although gazelles usually make off when the dogs are still more than 100 yards distant, zebra and wildebeest may allow them to close in this manner to within 50 or even 20 yards. According to David Houston, in an article in *Animals:*

If the game are in tight herds, the dogs will charge up to the group, running round and trying to get a single animal to leave the protection of its fellows. Once an animal has started to run, the whole pack will then give chase and remain united in the hunt, though one dog occasionally takes the place of another as leader, not being disturbed by other animals during the chase, even if the pack passes very close to them. Finally, as the pack catches up on the prey, it may spread out and cut off the routes of escape as the quarry starts swerving and running in a zigzag pattern.

The communal social organization of a pack of wild dogs is possibly even more remarkable than that of a pack of wolves, and a feature of this communalism is food sharing, for in con-

trast to the behavior of a pride of lions, instead of one dog
disputing another's place at a kill, all the members of a pack
usually feed peaceably together, bolting down chunks of flesh
before hyenas have time to assemble in strength to drive them
away. Moreover, a sick member of the pack arriving late at the
kill can obtain food by gnuzzling its nose into the corner of
another dog's mouth and stimulating regurgitation. As Houston
has pointed out, this suppression of aggressive instincts at a kill
is an essential adaptation to hunting in a pack, which has itself
obvious advantages over hunting solo; while the sharing of food
results in the fullest use being made of every kill. Furthermore,
from the time that the pups are strong enough to run with the
pack, and until they are about eight months old, it is usual for

Young Cape hunting dogs

the adults to stand aside and allow them to feed first, while keeping any straggler hyenas at bay. It has been suggested that the dogs' habit of holding their white-tipped tails erect when feeding serves to indicate the whereabouts of a kill to any young dogs that may have been outstripped during the course of a hunt. So diverse are the curious blotched markings of hunting dogs that these white "flags" are virtually the only color feature they have in common.

Finally, when the pack returns from hunting, food is regurgitated to the bitch that has remained at the den to guard the pups, and also direct to the latter, with the result that meat from a kill may enter several different stomachs before being finally digested—an arrangement that enables the pack to hunt at a considerable distance from its base. A bitch may indeed have difficulty in obtaining sufficient food for herself, so anxious are the dogs to disgorge to the pups, and equal difficulty in suckling them so effusively are they greeted and licked; while the pups may be unable to obtain milk from their mother because other bitches are suckling her!

Even more remarkable than the dogs' habit of food sharing is the fact that, if the single bitch in a pack dies, the dogs are able to rear the pups, with one taking her place on guard when the rest of the pack is away hunting. In one such instance an otherwise all-male pack of six dogs continued to bring food home to nine 5-week-old pups, and in another instance a pack of nine males cared for ten pups after the bitch had died, though only four of these survived to run with the pack. The relationships between the bitches in the pack seems to run counter to that between the dogs, and that between dogs and bitches, for some dominant bitches habitually persecute subordinate bitches and even kill their pups. In any pack of wild dogs there is apparently an excess of dogs over bitches, which in some packs is as great as ten to one. This imbalance serves to offset the fertility of the bitches, which are capable of producing several litters a year, with as many as sixteen pups in a litter. The wild dog population is further controlled by a high rate of mortality among the pups from predation by hyenas, and by the ravages of mange, rabies, the tick-borne parasite *Rickettsia canis*, and canine distemper, any of which may decimate entire packs during the hot months.

The only circumstances in which a pack settles in one locality for any length of time are when one of the bitches whelps in the abandoned earth of an aardvark or warthog or hyena. This usually occurs in March or April when game is abundant. When the dogs are not away hunting, they spend most of their time resting and sleeping near the den or in nearby burrows. From time to time one will wander over to greet the pups, which make their appearance at its entrance when three weeks old, and even go down into the den to lie with the pups for an hour while their mother lies in another hole. Jane van Lawick-Goodall has described how at one den three members of the pack emerged from their sleeping burrows almost at the same time, shortly after the sun had disappeared behind some heavy cloud at 4:30 in the afternoon, and headed for the pups' den, running along side by side, twittering like birds and licking and nibbling at each other's faces:

> One after the other they put their faces down the hole and whined, their ears pricked forward and their tails wagging. Suddenly [one of the bitches, not the pups' mother] rushed past them and right down into the den. I heard squeaking and twittering from the depths of the earth and then [the bitch] backed out, followed almost immediately by the eight pups.
>
> For several minutes there was confusion, as the adults greeted the pups and each other and, one by one, all the other

members of the pack appeared and joined in. But soon things calmed down, and the adult dogs lay down again and rested.

By the time that the pups are about six weeks old the pack is restless to resume its nomadic existence, no doubt because the game is becoming wary and moving out of their hunting territory, and there may be tentative attempts by other bitches in the pack to remove the pups to another den perhaps 40 yards distant, and subsequently to other dens, each of which may be occupied for a few days. The mother may also move the pups, even before they can walk, carrying them as much as 1000 yards to another refuge when lions are in the neighborhood. Although there is a report of a pack of eight dogs killing an adult male lion, they are as a general rule uneasy when lions are about, leaping up to look at them over the long grass, while uttering short hoarse barks. When the pups are eight or ten weeks old, however, and strong enough to hunt with the pack, the dogs finally resume their nomadic way of life.

17: The Trekbokke of the Springbok

The African savannas, like the steppes of Asia, merge into arid lands and semideserts, and are indeed themselves virtual desert during prolonged droughts. In eastern Kenya and Tanzania there are thousands of square miles of thorn thickets and very little grass, and because the annual rainfall is often less than 12 inches, the vegetation is adapted to near-desert conditions. The trunks of the umbrella acacias, for example, separate a few inches above ground level and the limbs spread to form a flat-topped crown at a height of 5 or 10 feet, with the result that, as Leslie Brown has pointed out, "The central grazing points are always protected from smaller browsing animals by the outer ring of the thorny branches, and the base of the tree is shaded from the rays of the sun, which may help to conserve water. The root system spreads out into open ground some distance from the tree."

To conserve moisture, trees shed their leaves after the rains, and during the long dry season the bush looks gray and dead. But though all the vegetation appears dead, the thorn trees, bristling with white spikes, are also preserving moisture, for if the few green buds are broken off, they are replaced by drops of sticky milk, with which the gerenuks satisfy their thirst. The bush is the habitat of browsing animals—elephants, black rhinos, giraffes, gerenuks, greater and lesser kudu, dik-dik, Grant's gazelles, impala—which either travel long distances to water or survive without it. However, the volume of dew in the bush may exceed that of the water, enabling impala, which teem from the deserts of northern Kenya to Tanzania, to disperse through the most arid country, while feeding on the beans in the pods of those acacias that ripen and fall during the dry season, and also on fallen marula apples, although in the wooded parts of the savannas they prefer fine grasses, when these are seasonally available. As Jane Burton has observed, the pods of most acacias are thin and papery, and burst while on the tree. The seeds shower onto the ground, the empty pods remain hanging on the tree:

> Browsing animals eat the pods, but do not pick up the scattered seeds from the ground below. However, the pods of *Acacia tortilis* do not burst. They are fleshy, large and heavy, and when ripe they fall to the ground without shedding their seeds. These pods have a strong smell which is very attractive to herbivores. Being rich in carbohydrates they form an important part of the dry season diet of impala and kudu, as well as of grass rats, which even put on fat at this season.
>
> In turn, the acacia is dependent on impala for the dispersal and germination of its seeds. When ungulates chew the pods, most of the hard, smooth, rounded seeds are not crushed and are also unharmed by their passage through the animal's gut. Indeed, they do not germinate unless they have passed through the gut of a ruminant. Two more species are closely

involved in this cycle: large mound-building termites and star-grass. Like impala, termites are dependent on this acacia for food; in some areas dead thorntrees are scattered all through *Acacia tortilis* country. On old or inactive termite hills grow star-grass, the grass which is most sought after by impala— who may manure it while eating it. Thus impala spread the acacia, the acacia feeds the impala and the termites; the termites encourage the star-grass, which also feeds the impala; the impala help to nourish the grass.

Just as the savannas of East Africa peter out in the northern deserts, so the South African veld merges with the Karoo. Eve Palmer has summed up the eastern Karoo, where 13 inches of rain fall in a very good year, but only 3 inches in a bad year, as at its worst a desert, at its best fine grazing, supporting all those desert antelope that can exist indefinitely without water where succulent plants are available. In between such times the Karoo is covered with low karoo bushes, perennial daisy bushes with long, thin, wandering roots and tiny tough leaves that survive where grass cannot, and succulents of many kinds:

> Away to the west the plains merge with the Great Karoo proper stretching three hundred miles to the Swartberg, the Black Mountains. . . . The summer heat of this wide upland world can . . . scarcely be imagined . . . soil too hot to walk on barefoot and rocks too hot to touch. . . . Rain, however rare, makes life possible. . . . Within days—hours it seems— the dust-dry soil is engulfed in succulence, every bare twig covered with leaves, the plains enamelled with flowers, the air filled with scents. The mountains cascade water, the rivers and pools brim over, frogs bellow, birds fill the trees, and bees make honey all over the countryside.

The Karoo will always be associated with what were possibly the greatest mass movements of any land animals—those of the springboks which grazed in millions over 1 million square miles

south of latitude 27½ and west of longitude 27½, though especially on the Karoo and in Bushman Land. When near the Great
Fish River in the 1840s, Gordon-Cumming wrote that "the plain
extended, without a break, until the eye could not discern any
object smaller than a castle, and throughout the whole of this extent were herds of thousands and tens of thousands of springboks, interspersed with troops of wildebeest."

The sporadic migrations or trekbokke of the springbok, which
were first described in 1782 by that flamboyant French ornithol-
ogist, Le Vaillant, originated in the north of what is now Cape
Province and went north in some years, south or west in other
years, sometimes crossing the mountains of Namaqualand en
route to the Atlantic Coast, sometimes traveling southward toward the Karoo and into near-desert country. The incredible
numbers of springbok taking part in these trekbokke do not appear to have been exaggerated, for their herds are reported to
have been so densely packed that larger antelope such as wildebeest and eland, and even lions, were carried along in their
flood, while domestic calves, sheep, and shepherd boys were
trampled to death. They never ran or trotted, but plodded
steadily on—as if hopper locusts said one eyewitness—with a
fixed unseeing look in their eyes, and apparently wholly un-
aware of men and predators killing among them. "If the front
ranks could not ford a stream," wrote Eve Palmer, "they were
pushed in by the buck behind and their bodies formed a bridge
for the multitude that followed."

According to the reliable Cronwright-Schreiner, the last of
four great trekbokke between 1887 and 1896 extended across a
front of 138 miles and was 15 miles deep, and the unbroken
mass of animals gave a whitish tint to the veld, as if there had
been a very light fall of snow. It was, as it happens, midwinter
at the time and freezing hard every night, for both the Karoo

and the Kalahari Desert were subject to long cold spells in winter, with severe frosts and snowstorms and jagged hail the size of cricket balls. One range of 80,000 acres was so eaten down and trampled by the springboks, possibly half a million, involved in this trekbokke that the entire stock of sheep and cattle had to be driven to another district.

T. B. Davie, who was born about 1837 in the Prieska District on the Orange River south of Griqualand, has described the 1887 trekbokke:

> When the trek was in full move nothing but springbok were to be seen for miles upon miles at a stretch . . . in one continuous stream, on the road and on both sides of the road, to the skyline, from the town of Prieska to Draghoender, a distance of 47 miles, plodding on, just moving aside far enough to avoid the wheels of a cart.
>
> On this occasion the owners of the farm Witvlei were all sitting in a ring round the top of the well, which at that time was uncovered, the father, son and son-in-law armed with rifles, firing a shot now and then, and the women folk with sticks and stones trying to keep the "boks" away. This was the family's only water supply left, as the "boks" had already filled up the dam, thousands being trampled to death in the mud as they pressed on over one another to get to the water. At last the "boks" beat the farmers and got to the well and in a few minutes it was full of dead and dying "boks". However, the trek passed before evening with the exception of a few stragglers. . . . In the course of a few days the trek seems to melt away.

This trekbokke, like an earlier one in 1860, in fact pressed on westward for more than 350 miles across Bushman Land and the mountains of Namaqualand until it reached the Atlantic Coast near the mouth of the Orange River, where the bodies of the vast numbers that were drowned while attempting to cross the estuary reputedly formed a barrier that extended for 30 miles along the beach. The following year Davie and a naturalist companion rode for 4½ miles straight through another trekbokke— "they never giving way more road than was required for us to pass"—and "guessed" that on the 10,000 acres within their view there were a hundred million springbok, without taking into account the additional millions on the miles of veld beyond their vision.

What factors triggered off these unpredictable trekbokke? Much of the springboks' habitat was arid and, in summer, scorching desert, moistened by perhaps only two or three rainstorms in the course of the year; while although the immense tracts of semidesert between the Orange River and Cape Colony contained ample brackish water and stagnant pools, there were no permanent springs, and the pools dried up during droughts, which occurred about one year in five. Nevertheless most of Bushman Land was covered with grass growing in thick shocks 30 inches high from raised tussocks 6 feet apart, while the Karoo provided grazing for millions of herbivores. So one's first impression is that some trekbokke, which were not in fact restricted to the springbok only, were instigated by a lack of water, though springbok can survive for very long periods without drinking; and during periods of total drought there was indeed a tendency for the game to begin a general migration away from the whole region.

In 1849, for example, Sir John G. Fraser, when living in Beaufort West (in the Karoo), where hardly anyone could recall a great trekbokke, described how after news had reached him of a severe drought in the interior, the inhabitants of the township were awakened one morning a week or two later "by a sound as of a strong wind before a thunderstorm, followed by the trampling of thousands of all kinds of game—wildebeest, blesboks, springboks, quaggas, elands, antelopes of all sorts and kinds (all in poor condition), which filled the streets and gardens, and as far as one could see covered the whole country, grazing off everything eatable . . . drinking up the waters in the street furrows, fountains and dams. . . . It took about three days before the whole of the trekbokke had passed, and it left our country looking as if a fire had passed over it."

But although the animals in some trekbokke were definitely in search of water, this was not invariably the case. Overgrazing, disease, or stress due to overcrowding may have been the causes in some instances, for though the members of some trekbokke were fat, they were more often in very poor condition and sometimes heavily infested with scab. Hunting pressures may also have brought about some dispersals, for Davie describes how in the Prieska District the springboks would wander aimlessly in mobs at irregular seasons but, after persistent hunting, eventually move off in one direction, usually toward the Orange River, though often southward; and Cronwright-Schreiner apparently drew a distinction between the migrant trekbokke springbok and the houbokke springbok which were permanently resident on one veld.

One further factor remains to be considered. The 1896 trekbokke did not disperse toward the Orange River, but migrated into the dry interior, where the does kidded. It was in fact not unusual for the does to give birth during the course of a trekbokke and, when the kids were strong enough, to return to their home range, providing that rain, which they were perhaps able to smell at a great distance, had fallen during their absence. Alternatively, they remained in the interior for a further year and kidded a second time. This behavior suggests a dispersal in search of forage, and W. C. Scully, who was a magistrate in up-country South Africa from 1876 to 1899 and witnessed the last great trekbokke across Great Bushmanland from east to west in 1892, believed that the Bushman Land springbok migrated from the interior during the rainless winter, in order to kid on its western coastal fringes, where soaking rain showers in the early winter produced a rich vegetation on the sandy plains for a few weeks. After kidding, they slowly returned to their home range where some rain fell during the summer months: "All night long the muffled thunder of their hoofs could be heard, whilst clouds of dust hung motionless in the dew-damp air."

Why did trekbokke on the grand scale terminate in 1896? There are a number of possible reasons. From that year until at least as late as 1916 there was, for example, a widespread drying up of pans and water holes; there was extensive agricultural development of the veld, associated with settlement and the fencing off of immense areas; there were outbreaks of rinderpest, from which nearly all the animals in the 1896 trekbokke were reported to have died; there were severe hunting pressures. A combination of all these factors perhaps has reduced the once colossal population of springbok to small, virtually nonmigratory herds in the Kalahari's Gemsbok National Park and in a few other localities such as the Etosha Pans and North Amboland.

18: Survival in African Deserts

More than one-fifth of Africa is arid, though its deserts or semi-deserts may take the form of rocky plateaus, glittering white salt pans, or areas the size of France of shifting sand dunes or ergs. Ergs up to 700 feet high, cresent-shaped where sand is relatively scarce, sword-shaped where winds are variable, cover a seventh of the Sahara—the *Sahra*, the dull brown wilderness or emptiness of the Arabs, extending for 3000 miles from east to west, and more than 1000 miles from north to south, but itself only a part of the Great Palearctic Desert that stretches from the Atlantic to northern India and central China.

But regions designated as desert on maps are not necessarily true desert in reality. The French Sahara, for example, includes mountainous country supporting nomad peoples and their camels; even the immense sand dunes of the Arabian Nefud bear grass and scrub; while though ground temperatures in the Kalahari reach 161° F, it is desert only in the sense that it contains no permanent surface water whatever. In other respects the Kalahari is a steppe desert supporting a large nomadic fauna, for its long lines of sand dunes, 100 to 150 feet apart, stained pink or red or maroon with iron oxide, are crested with stiff grasses, whitish during drought, green after rain; and there are regions where the landscape is almost parklike. In *The Lost World of the Kalahari*, Laurens van der Post portrayed it as an Eden of "deep fertile sands covered with grass, glistening in the wind like fields of gallant corn, luxuriant bush, clumps of trees, and in places great strips of its own dense woods; and when the rains come . . . sweet-tasting grasses and . . . bushes with amber berries, glowing raisins, sugared plums." More prosaically, the sand ridges and the valleys between them are sparsely covered with grasses and shrubs, and when grass is scarce there is forage on the black and gray camel thorns, which grow as stunted shrubs on the dunes and as groves of shady trees in riverbeds where, although water is a rare phenomenon, moisture lies within reach of their roots. As in the northern thorn scrub, so in the Kalahari these trees bear nutritious pods, and Van der Post has described how after the rains there is a great invasion of life from the outside world:

> Every bird, beast and indigenous being waits expectantly on its stony upland for the summer to come round. . . . As soon as the air goes dank with a whiff of far-off water they will wait no longer. The elephant is generally the first to move in. . . . Close on his heels follow numbers of buck (gemsbok, springbok, eland), wildebeest, zebra, and the carnivorous beasts (lion and leopard) that live off them. Even the black buffalo emerges from the river-beds and swamps shaking the tsetse fly like flakes of dried clay from his coat, and grazes in surly crescents far into the desert.

This invasion of game is probably responsible for the dispersion and germination of the desert's plant seeds, and also for those of the essential moisture-containing tsama melons, which make life possible not only for the antelopes and equines, but also for elephant, rhino, jackals, rodents, and even lions.

The presence of lions in semidesert is particularly noteworthy, for in their more usual habitats they are never farther than 5 or 10 miles from water, without which they cannot apparently survive for longer than a few days. In the Kalahari they are known to dig up watermelons, but there are no melons in the Haud country, on the border between Somalia and Abyssinia, which may be totally waterless for months at a time, nor in northwest Kordofan in the Sudan, where water is present only in isolated wells at depths of 30 or 40 feet.

On the southern borders of the Sahara, where air temperatures can be as high as 118° F and ground temperatures 158° F, lions must exist in similar conditions, and in Wadi Hawar, 300 miles west-northwest of Khartoum in the desert of northern Sudan, they lie up during the heat of the day in "burrows" under shady acacias. One such den examined by Michael Mason had originally been an aardvark burrow, two of the four entrances to which the lions had enlarged. Within 30 yards of the den were hundreds of skulls, horns, hooves, and hides of addax antelope and dorcas and addra gazelles, together with the feathers of ostriches. In such regions the lions no doubt obtain sufficient liquid from the blood and water present in the bodies of their prey, just as the gazelles, which may be more than 300 miles from the nearest water, obtain both food and water exclusively from acacia bushes, whose leaves have a 60 percent water content even in drought conditions.

In an article in *Animals*, Dudley D'Ewes has described how any year's crop of tsama melons is always found in the path of the previous year's rainstorms, and most rainfall in the Kalahari takes the form of localized thunderstorms or of wind-driven showers that follow fairly narrow random paths:

Game animals with access to enough melons can do without drinking-water, so in the dry season they follow the ripe melons that spring up along the storms' routes. Because of the rain, these same areas where there are melons will obviously carry a healthy stand of grass and a good crop of fruit on the trees and shrubs, as well as a full array of leaves on nutritious shrubs. . . . On the other hand the country in between these areas, where the previous year brought no rain, will be dry and bare . . . except the tough stubs of tussocky dune grasses. So animals free to roam will avoid these places and concentrate on areas where food is available. This is a sort of built-in safety device in tender country like the Kalahari. The animals go where the veld is able to carry them and stay away from the areas that they would trample bare and leave vulnerable to wind erosion.

If there is an abundant crop of melons and other large succulent roots that are to be found 8 or 9 inches below the surface in the driest parts of the dunes, and for which elephants plow up whole tracts with their tusks, herds of sixty or seventy gemsbok can remain on the sandhills throughout the dry season. Gemsbok are the main prey of lions and spotted hyenas in the Kalahari, though a buck is capable of killing a lion with its long, straight, sharp-pointed horns. They resemble (though much larger than) the northern beisa oryx that graze in herds of two hundred or more on the grassy steppes, interspersed with thorn, rising from the edge of Ethiopia's Danakil Desert—that immense block of salt, 140 miles long by 40 miles wide and half a mile thick, much of it below sea level, resulting from the evaporation of a volcanic-caused lake

Within the Danakil there is no life, either plant or animal, except for the camel caravans carrying salt, attended by scavenging Egyptian vultures. The beisa share the steppes with kudu and gazelles, and are accompanied by carmine bee-eaters of the northern race which, instead of preying on bees like the other fourteen species of African bee-eaters, feed on grasshoppers and locusts. Because these insects are difficult to see in the long grass, the bee-eaters ride on the backs of the beisa, and also the bustards, that flush them. Until World War II thousands of white oryx and also gazelles grazed the ephemeral pastures of short wiry grass that sprang up after rain on the sand and gravel plains of the Arabian deserts, obtaining moisture from dew and roots, but the exploitation of oil introduced mechanized hunting to the desert, in the form of helicopters and fleets of automobiles, three hundred in line. This has almost or wholly exterminated the oryx, and none have been reported since October 1972.

The scarcity of water in the habitats of gemsbok and oryx is accentuated by the conditions of low humidity and extreme temperatures, and it is possible that some oryx never drink water throughout their lives. To conserve moisture they probably sweat little and pass highly concentrated urine, while the glossy coats of the Arabian oryx are thick enough to insulate them against the sun's heat. One may also ask, how is it possible for oryx to stand in the desert sun hour after hour without suffering heatstroke? In offering a solution to this problem, Norman Myers has pointed out, in *The Long African Day*, that the area inside an oryx's skull stays substantially cooler than the rest of its body:

> The blood supply to the brain flows along the carotid artery, passing on the way through the "cavernous sinus" region made up of hundreds of tiny parallel arteries. Coursing through the sinus area from the other direction is venous blood on its way back to the heart after passing through the

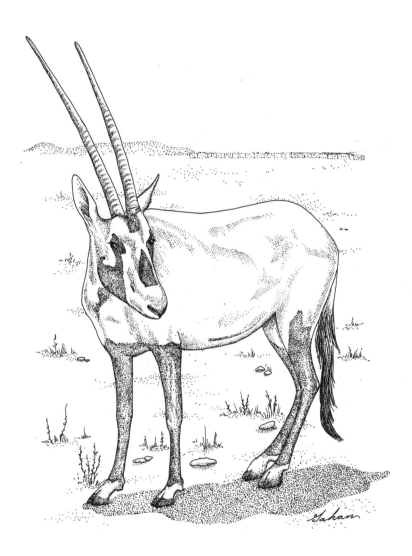

Arabian oryx

nasal passages, where it has been cooled by evaporation in the respiratory tracts. The arterial blood of the carotid then flows on to the brain a good six degrees cooler than when it was pumped out of the heart.

By far the most extensive areas of sand dunes in the world's deserts lie within the Libyan Desert, which is comparable in size and configuration with India, and more particularly in the Great Sand Sea of western Egypt, where whaleback sand ridges, 20 or 60 miles long, lie side by side like, in Bagnold's words in *Libyan Sands*, "an infinite raft of logs, along each of which grew . . . dunes like notched caterpillars end to end in continuous chains." Throughout the greater part of the interior of the Libyan Desert the only sign of life to the casual observer, apart from an infrequent bird of prey, is that of small migrant birds, dead or soon to die—relics from the host that cross North Africa on a broad front in the course of their migrations to and from Europe and Asia, though Mason noted in a number of localities that when rain stimulated a growth of grass, after a drought that might have lasted for twenty years, gerbils suddenly appeared, despite the fact that there was no other vegetation within 200 or 300 miles. The only source of water is oasis depressions, often several hundred miles apart, deep enough to tap artesian upwellings, and such oases attract desert foxes and jerboas, lizards and snakes and, if not more than 20 miles apart, gazelles. At the extreme limits of vegetation in the desert, small herds of addax forage. As shy as the gazelles are tame, they are equipped with skin an inch thick on the nape to afford some protection against the sun, and with inner lips, resembling several rows of soft-toothed combs, to sift the sand from their food.

A contributor to *The Living Animals of the World* has stated that in less arid regions the relatively high humidity of the air surrounding the loose grains of sand at a depth of 20 inches is of crucial importance to burrowing animals. The temperature of the sand in Wadi Halfa in the Sudan, for example, can be as high as 183° F, but at a depth of 20 inches there is only the slightest variation between day and night temperatures of 60° or 65° F, while at twice that depth the annual range of temperature is only 18 degrees. Consider the Sudanese jerboa, weighing only 2 or 3 ounces, with a 9-inch tail 3 inches longer than its body. It lives alone in its burrow in the summer and in pairs in the winter, though numbers gather to "play" at night at a special burrow with a larger entrance. It does not find it necessary either to hibernate or aestivate, for it forages for seeds and dried grasses only after the sun has set. From this dry feed, it, like other desert rodents, manufactures all the liquid it requires, for although it eats sprouting vegetation during the rainy season, and succulent roots when there is no rain, it can exist without fresh vegetation for a year or longer and does not, unlike the gerbil, store food.

During the heat of the day in summer the jerboa seals its burrow with a plug of soft sand, thereby excluding hot air—and possibly also snakes. On emerging at night it breaks through the plug with its head, remaining with head only aboveground until satisfied that it is safe to come out. Then it pushes the sand back into the mouth of the burrow and turns around and pats the sand with its flat muscular nose until the entrance is almost invisible. Because a jerboa has no sweat glands, and therefore cannot lose heat by sweating and cannot afford to lose fluids in order to keep cool, it is essential that it does not become overheated. Writing of the jerboa in the western Egyptian desert, J. P. Kirmiz noted that it can control the temperature and humidity of its burrow in three different ways:

(a) by modifying the length and depth of the burrow; (b) by

controlling the extent of the soil seal which closes its entrance; and (c) by providing cotton wool for winter months. . . . During the very hours when the blazing summer sun, with its intensity of radiation, heats the ground and the air above it to intolerable degrees of temperature and dryness, the jerboa's cool and humid burrow provides an ideal place for rest and sleep in the desert. Also at times when desert storms of wind, sand and rain become extremely trying to living creatures above the ground, the jerboa's burrow is a safe refuge.

He continues:

The comfortable microclimate which the jerboa has created for itself in the midst of the desert, and in which it lives, is its burrow. Anatomically equipped with a pair of hands, each of which has five fingers ending in thin and sharp claws, the jerboa digs fast and deep into the desert sand and clay, using its hands, nose, head and long hind-limbs with highly co-ordinated movements. The soil so dug is either brushed away with the brush-like hairy toes of its hind-limbs or pushed out with the hands, nose and head, or beaten with the nose and head to solidify the sides of the tunnel. . . .

For the rainy winter days the jerboa digs its burrow on the slope of hills to avoid inundation by rain. For the summer it prepares its burrow on less elevated areas, near the edges of open fields, where some vegetation is found.

The end of each burrow forms a spherical abode of about 15 cm. diameter. . . . This nest contains canvas wool in winter months to help the jerboa to keep warm. The wool is prepared by the animal from any piece of jute or cloth that it may find in the fields. Its fine fingers and nails are adept in tearing apart any piece of cloth to make of it the finest heap of wool within a few hours.

The largest single area in the world devoid of vegetation, outside glacial polar regions, are the salt deserts of Iran; but even in extremely arid regions, such as the central Sahara or the Libyan desert, desiccated vegetation, blown and tumbled over the sands by winds from the desert edges for scores or hundreds of miles until finally coming to rest, harbors small populations of insects, spiders, and scorpions. We may consider the most remarkable desert insects to be locusts, though to be strictly accurate even the desert locust, *Schistocerea gregaris*, whose distribution is roughly coincident with hot Palearctic deserts, is not a typical desert insect, since it is normally restricted to the sand dunes of the coastal plains and to belts of scrub along the beds of wadis, roosting in shrubs and trees at night and feeding mainly on annual and perennial plants. There are fewer than ten species of true locusts, which are structurally similar to grasshoppers, and in the ordinary course of events desert locusts are solitary and behave like relatively harmless grasshoppers.

The females deposit their twenty to one hundred eggs, glued together by means of a secretion in the shape of a cone, at a depth of 4 or 5 inches in sand that is dry on the surface but damp beneath, and the nymphs or hoppers hatch after thirty-five to fifty days—though the brown locust of the Karoo lays in bone-dry soil, and its eggs may remain in the soil for perhaps two years until sufficient rain falls to stimulate hatching; but if there is a scarcity of green vegetation, large numbers of females concentrate in a few areas to lay their eggs in close proximity, with the result that overcrowding triggers off changes in hormone production. This results in the birth of a generation of black and orange hoppers which, remarkably, differ not only in color and form from the vivid green solitary hoppers, but also in behavior, since they are gregarious. After hatching, they gather into swarms of hundreds, thousands, or millions, and set out on their devastating travels, devouring every blade of green vegetation during the course of five successive molts.

On the South African veld these *roodi-baatjes* (red-jackets) or *voetgangers* (footsloggers), as the Boers called them, clustered in bushes at night—every little karoo bush for miles and miles packed with them. In the morning they descended to bask in the sun, lying at an angle to expose their bodies to the maximum heat, before hopping on in great columns across the veld, advancing possibly a quarter of a mile in an hour in hops of an inch or two at a time, very much less than the distance they can jump. At the appearance of small birds, which preyed on the outliers, they banded together in masses, but dispersed over the veld to escape large birds such as storks, climbing up into the bushes again when the ground became too hot. Nearly always they followed tracks and paths in narrow columns, marching in one direction one behind the other, over or through almost any obstacle.

In describing a locust invasion of Sinai, C. S. Jarvis wrote in *Three Deserts* that "Looking at a swarm of hoppers crawling across the desert is like watching a slow steady inundation by a black flood, as the insects follow every depression in the ground, and when the undulating mass with its uniform forward movement comes to a patch of country with hummocks dotted here and there, the line swirls inwards into fast-running streams, passes through the channels between the hummocks and then, with its constant trickling motion, spreads out again across the flat."

Cronwright-Schreiner describes one practically unbroken swarm, some *40 miles* in depth, which passed through the town of Cradock in the Karoo:

Down the streets the hopping locusts came. . . . They filled and devoured the gardens and swarmed into open doors and went through the houses. . . . They streamed into the hotel; I saw them going up the stairway . . . as I passed the open upstairs window, where many were sitting on the sills, they just jumped out into the air!

After their fifth molt the hoppers metamorphose into adult winged insects, approximately 1½ inches long. Their initial flights are short, but soon become longer, and they finally leave their hatching areas in inconceivably colossal swarms that may extend over an area of 2000 square miles. Karen Blixen has described how at times a small swarm would come along, a free corps which had detached itself from the main force, and would just pass in a rush:

> But at other times the grasshoppers came in big flights which took days to pass over the farm, twelve hours' incessant hurling advance in the air. When the flight was at its highest it was like a blizzard at home, whistling and shrieking like a high wind, little hard furious wings to all sides of you and over your head, shining like thin blades of steel in the sun, but themselves darkening the sun.

These long-distance migrations of swarms containing an average of perhaps a thousand million locusts, consuming daily about 3000 tons of green food, were conducted at a height where wind speeds were often greater than the insects' maximum flight speed, with the result that their swarms tended to be windborne into areas of low barometric pressure, where rain was most likely to fall, and where they would be able to feed on ephemeral grasses that sprouted with the rain, and subsequently deposit their eggs in sand that was suitably damp beneath. As Leslie Brown has pointed out, in northeast Africa three differing periods of rainfall coalesce in a comparatively small area, with the result that locusts can breed in almost any month of the year; and during the five or six months of their migratory phase, each of the millions of females lays several times, producing a total aggregate of between three hundred and a thousand eggs during her lifetime.

In the end, however, these enormous temporary populations

of locusts, some of which have migrated 3000 miles, are decimated by insect parasites such as sarcophagus flies that lay their eggs not only on the locusts' eggs, but also on the locusts themselves at the juncture of head and thorax; by famine and lack of shelter; and by inclement weather. "There is no doubt," wrote J. L. Cloudsley-Thompson in his *Life in Deserts*, "that the instability of the environment and, in particular, the unreliability of rainfall in desert regions makes the life of the locusts very precarious. But its mobility, linked as it is with weather dynamics, helps it to overcome its physiological handicaps."

Selected Bibliography

Adamson, George. *Bwana Game.* London: Collins & Harvill, 1968. (Published in the United States as *A Lifetime with Lions.* Garden City, N.Y.: Doubleday, 1968.)

Adamson, Joy. *Born Free.* New York: Pantheon; London: Harvill, 1960.

———. *Forever Free.* London: Collins & Harvill, 1962; New York: Harcourt, Brace & World, 1963.

———. *Living Free.* New York: Harcourt, Brace & World; London: Collins & Harvill, 1961.

———. *The Spotted Sphinx.* New York: Harcourt, Brace & World; London: Collins & Harvill, 1969.

Allen, Durward L. *The Life of Prairies and Plains.* New York: McGraw-Hill, 1967.

Allen, J. A. "The American Bison, Living and Extinct." *Memoirs of the Museum of Comparative Zoology* 4, 10 (1876).

Ames, Evelyn. *A Glimpse of Eden.* Boston: Houghton Mifflin, 1967; London: Collins, 1968.

Andrews, Roy Chapman. "Living Animals of the Gobi Desert." *Natural History* 24 (1924): 150–59.

Bagnold, Ralph A. *Libyan Sands: Travel in a Dead World.* London: Hodder and Stoughton, 1935.

Bannikov, A. G. *Biology of the Saiga.* Jerusalem: Israel Program for Scientific Translation, 1961.
———. "The Saga of the Saiga." *Animals* 12, 6 (1969): 244–48.
Bere, Rennie. "Freedom Is Confined." *Animals* 3, 11 (1964): 290–93.
Blixen, Karen. *See* Dinesen, Isak.
Bourlière, François, and Editors of *Life. The Land and Wildlife of Eurasia.* New York: Time, Inc., 1964.
Breeden, Stanley, and Breeden, Kay. "Dwellers of the Gibber Plain." *Animals* 9, 5 (1966): 314–17.
Breeden, Stanley, and Slater, Peter. *Birds of Australia.* New York: Taplinger; London: Angus & Robertson, 1968.
Brehm, Alfred Edmund. *From North Pole to Equator: Studies of Wild Life and Scenes in Many Lands.* Translated by Margaret R. Thomson. London: Blackie, 1896.
Brooks, Alan. *A Study of Thomson's Gazelle.* London: Her Majesty's Stationery Office, 1959.
Brown, Leslie. *Africa: A Natural History.* New York: Random House; London: Hamish Hamilton, 1965.
———. *The Life of the African Plains.* New York: McGraw-Hill, 1972.
Burton, Jane. *Animals of the African Year: The Ecology of East Africa.* New York: Holt, Rinehart & Winston; London: Peter Lowe, 1972.
Burton, Maurice. *Animals of Europe: The Ecology of Wildlife.* New York: Holt, Rinehart & Winston; London: Peter Lowe, 1973.
Buxton, P. A. *Animal Life in Deserts.* New York: Longmans, Green; London: Edward Arnold, 1923.
Cahalane, Victor H. *Mammals of North America.* New York: Macmillan, 1947, 1966.
Carr, Archie, and Editors of *Life. The Land and Wildlife of Africa.* New York: Time-Life International (Nederland), 1964.
Carr, Norman. *Return to the Wild: A Story of Two Lions.* New York: E. P. Dutton; London: Collins, 1962.
———. *The White Impala: The Story of a Game Ranger.* London: Collins, 1969.
Carruthers, Douglas. *Beyond the Caspian: A Naturalist in Central Asia.* Edinburgh: Oliver & Boyd, 1949.
———. *Unknown Mongolia: A Record of Travel and Exploration in North-West Mongolia and Dzungaria.* London: Hutchinson, 1913.
Catlin, George. *Letters and Notes on the Manners, Customs, and Conditions of the North American Indians.* 2 vols. London: Author, 1841.
Cloudsley-Thompson, J. L., and Chadwick, M. J. *Life in Deserts.*

Chester Springs, Pa.: Dufour Editions; London: G. T. Foulis, 1964.

Costello, David F. *The Prairie World*. New York: Thomas Y. Crowell, 1969; Newton Abbot: David & Charles, 1971.

Cowie, Isaac. *The Company of Adventurers. On the Great Buffalo Plains.* Toronto: William Briggs, 1913.

Cowie, Mervyn. *The African Lion*. New York: Golden Press; London: Arthur Barker, 1966.

Crisler, Lois. *Arctic Wild*. New York: Harper & Brothers, 1958, 1973; London: Secker & Warburg, 1959.

Cronwright-Schreiner, S. C. *The Migratory Springbucks of South Africa*. London: T. Fisher Unwin, 1925.

Cullen, Anthony. *Window onto Wilderness*. Kenya: East African Publishing House, 1969.

Dary, David A. *The Buffalo Book: The Full Saga of the American Animal*. Chicago: The Swallow Press, 1974.

D'Ewes, Dudley. "Animals Can Make Deserts." *Animals* 4, 3 (1964): 58–63.

Dinesen, Isak. *Out of Africa*. London: Putnam, 1937; New York: Random House, 1938.

Dodge, Richard Irving. *Our Wild Indians*. Hartford, Conn.: Worthington & Co., 1883.

————. *The Plains of the Great West*. New York: G. P. Putnam, 1877.

Douglas-Hamilton, Ian, and Douglas-Hamilton, Oria. *Among the Elephants*. London: Collins & Harvill, 1965.

Durrell, Gerald. *The Whispering Land*. London: Rupert Hart-Davis, 1961; New York: Viking, 1962.

Eiseley, Loren. *The Unexpected Universe*. New York: Harcourt, Brace & World, 1969; London: Victor Gollancz, 1970.

Erize, Francisco. "Patagonian 'Mares.' " *Animals*, 13, 12 (1971): 548–49.

Farnham, Thomas J. *Travels in the Great Western Prairies, 1839*. Poughkeepsie, N.Y.: Killey and Lossing, 1841; London: Richard Bentley, 1843.

Finlayson, H. H. *The Red Centre: Man and Beast in the Heart of Australia*. Sydney: Angus & Robertson, 1935.

Fosbrooke, Henry. *Ngorongoro: The Eighth Wonder*. London: Andre Deutsch, 1972.

Frame, George W. "The Black Rhinoceros." *Animals* 13, 15 (1971): 693–99.

Fuente, Felix Rodriguez de la. *Hunters and Hunted of the Savannah.* Translated by John Gilbert. London: Orbis, 1971.

Gordon-Cumming, Roualeyn George. *The Lion Hunter in South Africa.* London: John Murray, 1856.

Groves, Colin P. *Horses, Asses and Zebras in the Wild.* Hollywood, Fla.: Ralph Curtis Books; Newton Abbot: David & Charles, 1974.

Guggisberg, C. A. W. *Giraffes.* London: Arthur Barker, 1969.

———. *Simba: The Life of the Lion.* London: Bailey Bros. & Swinfen, 1962; Philadelphia: Chilton, 1963.

———. "Wild Dogs of the Savannah." *Animals* 1, 24 (1963): 4–7.

Haviland, Maud D. *Forest, Steppe and Tundra: Studies in Animal Environment.* New York and Cambridge: Cambridge University Press, 1926.

Hind, Henry Youle. *Narrative of the Canadian Red River Exploring Expedition of 1857.* London: Longmans, Green, Longman & Roberts, 1960; Rutland, Vt.: C. E. Tuttle, 1971.

Houston, David. "Hunting Dogs of East Africa." *Animals* 11, 11 (1969): 506–9.

Hudson, W. H. *Birds of La Plata.* New York: E. P. Dutton; London: J. M. Dent, 1920.

———. *Far Away and Long Ago.* New York: E. P. Dutton; London: J. M. Dent, 1918.

———. *The Naturalist in La Plata.* New York: E. P. Dutton; London: J. M. Dent, 1923.

Jaeger, Edmund C. *The North American Deserts.* Stanford, Calif.: Stanford University Press, 1957.

Jarvis, C. S. *Three Deserts.* London: John Murray, 1936.

Jones, Frederic Wood. *The Mammals of South Australia.* Adelaide: Government Printer, 1923.

Keast, Allen. *Australia and the Pacific Islands: A Natural History.* New York: Random House; London: Hamish Hamilton, 1966.

Kirmiz, J. P. *Adaptation to Desert Environment: A Study on the Jerboa, Rat and Man.* New York: Plenum; London: Butterworth, 1962.

Kruuk, Hans. *The Spotted Hyena: A Study of Predation and Social Behavior.* Chicago and London: The University of Chicago Press, 1972.

Lawick-Goodall, Hugo van. *Solo.* London: Collins, 1973; Boston: Houghton Mifflin, 1974.

———, and Jane van. *Innocent Killers.* London: Collins, 1970; Boston: Houghton Mifflin, 1971.

Lawick-Goodall, Jane van. "Vultures That Use Tools." *Animals* 12, 3 (1969): 100–5.

Le Souef, A. S. *The Wild Animals of Australasia.* London: George G. Harrap, 1926.

Mason, Michael H. *The Paradise of Fools: Being an account, by a member of the party, of the Expedition which covered 6,300 miles of the Libyan Desert by motor-car in 1935.* London: Hodder and Stoughton, 1936.

Matthews, L. Harrison. *British Mammals.* New York: British Book Centre; London: Collins, 1952.

Mech, L. David. *The Wolf: The Ecology and Behavior of an Endangered Species.* Garden City, N.Y.: American Museum of Natural History, 1970.

Merriam, C. Hart. *The Prairie Dog of the Great Plains. Yearbook* of the United States Department of Agriculture, 1901. Washington: Government Printing Office, 1902.

Mohr, Erna. *The Asiatic Wild Horse.* Translated by Daphne Machin Goodall. London: J. A. Allen, 1971.

Montagu, Ivor. "The Wild Bactrian." *Animals* 3, 1 (1963): 2–5.

Moore, Audrey. *Serengeti.* London: Country Life, 1938; New York: Charles Scribner's Sons, 1939.

Murie, Adolph. *A Naturalist in Alaska.* New York: Doubleday, 1963.

Myers, Norman. *The Long African Day.* New York: Macmillan, 1972; London: Cassell, 1973.

Nelson, Bryan. *Azraq: A Desert Oasis.* London: Allen Lane, 1973; Athens: Ohio University Press, 1974.

Palmer, Eve. *The Plains of Camdeboo.* London: Collins, 1966; New York: Viking, 1967.

Perk, Kalman. "How Camels Survive." *Animals* 5, 20 (1965): 550–53.

Pfeffer, Pierre. *Asia: A Natural History.* New York: Random House; London: Hamish Hamilton, 1968.

Pizzey, Graham. *Animals and Birds in Australia.* Melbourne: Cassell Australia, 1966.

———. "Journey into the Outback." *Animals* 8, 4 (1965): 86–91.

Przewalski, Nikolai Mikhailovich. *From Kulja, Across the Tian Shan to Lob-Nor.* London: Sampson Low, Marston, Searle & Rivington, 1879.

Ratcliffe, Francis. *Flying Fox and Drifting Sand: The Adventures of a Biologist in Australia.* New York: Medill McBride, 1938; London: Angus & Robertson, 1947.

Reader's Digest Association. *The Living World of Animals.* New York and London: Reader's Digest Association, 1970.

Rijke, A. M. "The Water-Holding Mechanism of Sandgrouse Feathers." *Journal of Experimental Biology* 56 (1972): 195–200.

Roe, Frank Gilbert. *The North American Buffalo. A Critical Study of the Species in Its Wild State.* Toronto: University Press, 1970; Newton Abbot: David & Charles, 1972.

Sanderson, Ivan T. *The Natural Wonders of North America.* London: Hamish Hamilton, 1962.

Schaller, George B. *Serengeti: A Kingdom of Predators.* New York: Knopf, 1972; London: Collins, 1973.

————. *The Serengeti Lion: A Study of Predator-Prey Relations.* Chicago: University of Chicago Press, 1972.

Schanensee, R. M. de. *A Guide to the Birds of South America.* Edinburgh: Oliver & Boyd, 1972.

Schenkel, Rudolf, and Schenkel-Hulliger, Lotte. *Ecology and Behaviour of the Black Rhinoceros: A Field Study.* Hamburg and Berlin: Paul Parey, 1969.

Schmidt-Nielsen, Knut. *Desert Animals: Physiological Problems of Heat and Water.* New York and London: Oxford University Press, 1964.

Scully, William Charles. *Further Reminiscences of a South African Pioneer.* London: T. Fisher Unwin, 1913.

Serventy, Vincent. *The Singing Land: Twenty-two Natural Environments of Australia.* London: Angus & Robertson, 1972; New York: Charles Scribner's Sons, 1974.

Seton, Ernest Thompson. *Life-Histories of Northern Animals.* 2 vols. London: Constable, 1910.

Sharland, Michael. *A Territory of Birds.* London: Angus & Robertson, 1964.

Sheldrick, Daphne. *The Tsavo Story.* London: Collins & Harvill, 1973.

Simon, Trevor. "Hyenas in the Ngorongoro." *Animals* 11, 4 (1968): 170–73.

Stevenson-Hamilton, J. *Wild Life in South Africa.* London: Cassell, 1947.

Sturt, Charles. *Narrative of an Expedition into Central Australia (1844–46).* London: T. and W. Boone, 1849.

Tegner, Henry. *Wild Hares.* London: John Baker, 1969.

Townsend, John K. *Narrative of a Journey across the Rocky Mountains.* Philadelphia: Henry Perkins, 1839.

Troughton, Ellis. *Furred Animals of Australia.* London: Angus & Robertson, 1941; Narberth, Pa.: Livingston, 1966.

Van der Post, Laurens. *The Lost World of the Kalahari.* New York: William Morrow; London: Hogarth Press, 1958.

Walker, Lewis Wayne. "The American Desert." *Animals* 3, 12 (1964): 309–15.

————. "The World's Smallest Owls." *Animals* 5, 20 (1965): 544.

Wetmore, A. "Observations on the Birds of Argentina, Paraguay and Chile." Smithsonian Institution *Bulletin*. U.S. National Museum 133 (1926): 1–434.

Young, Stanley P. *The Clever Coyote*. Washington, D.C.: Wildlife Management Institute, 1951.

Zalensky, V. *Przewalski's Horse*. London: Hurst & Blackett, 1907.

Index